FACES OF THE *New* FEMININE LEADERSHIP

Real Women. *Real* Conversations. *Real* Impact.

By TRACEY TROTTENBERG *with*

KRISTY DEEGAN   LEANNE DISANTO   LISA MARGULIES
ALLISON WATTS   ALYSSA RIZZO   STEFFI JO   SHARYN HENRY

Faces of the New Feminine Leadership

by Tracey Trottenberg with Kristy Deegan, Alyssa Rizzo, Allison Watts, Leanne DiSanto, Sharyn Henry, Steffi Jo, & Lisa Margulies

ISBN: 978-1-944177-25-6 (p)
ISBN: 978-1-944177-26-3 (e)

Crescendo Publishing, LLC
300 Carlsbad Village Drive
Ste. 108A, #443
Carlsbad, California 92008-2999

www.CrescendoPublishing.com
GetPublished@CrescendoPublishing.com

A Gift for You

https://youtu.be/DTFzaj-UTtk

As a way of expressing our gratitude for your purchase, many of the Amazing Women Authors have created a special gift for you. Our desire is that you find your story as you read through ours, discover more about yourself as you witness our journey, and find the courage to bring forward your voice to make a greater impact.

Enjoy the book and please enjoy this special gift I have here for you so you can take the action to get your message out and fulfill the calling inside of you that you're meant to share with the world.

Go to: www.amazingwomen.org/faces

Dedication

This book is dedicated to You: the woman yearning to share your deepest heart and express more of yourself to make a bigger difference. You are safe to step out and be seen, and we have your back. We're all in this together, and the women in this book are leading first and sharing what's possible. There are people who need your unique voice and message. There are lives that you are uniquely meant to impact and touch, including your own. The lives of other women, men, children and animals are waiting for all of us, including you, to bring peace and kindness as we lead with love. There is a place inside of you that knows it's time to shine your light as brightly as you are meant, and show up for your divine duty. We know it too, and this is for you.

This book is dedicated to the men in our lives and in our community. You are strong and courageous. We love you, and are so very grateful for your support as we shine bright. We are in partnership with you. Your bravery and heroic willingness to fan our flames keeps us feeling safe and fearless in our unshakable stand. We write and share this in Oneness with you.

This book is dedicated to all the children of the world who carry the light within and are ready for humanity to change our ways, and our conversations. We are sharing our journeys and hard-earned truth to nurture and clear the way for an easier path for you. We share our voice so you can feel more safe and inspired as we all help to bring our world into balance, kindness, caring and love.

This book is dedicated to the compassion for the process of what it means to be human and what it takes to wake up to the Truth of who we are. It is the journey, not the destination, which allows us to embrace all of who we are here to be as we grow into greater self-expression. It requires tremendous courage and self-care to love ourselves first and be supported in community so we can all grow together. Our language and consciousness in how we communicate is the key. As we learn to accept and celebrate ourselves and others, we truly do bring heaven to earth right now. We embrace the messiness of the journey, and our own perfect imperfections. Together, we play full out to make the most of this magnificent life we have.

Finally and most importantly, this book is dedicated to whatever higher power we acknowledge and know (whatever your word is: God/Spirit/Source/Universe/_____). Each of us here as a co-author is available to be used fully and for a greater purpose. We offer our stories, our love and our leadership in service to the highest possibility for all humankind.

Love for Faces of the New Feminine Leadership

"It takes a village to raise a child, and it takes a village to support a woman's courage to free her voice. I've seen the transformation that happens when a woman unleashes her spirit and leads with love. This book is the village and each woman's story is her freedom to make a bigger impact."

Cynthia Kersey,
Founder and CEO, Unstoppable Foundation

"The journeys these women share illuminate what it takes to move beyond pain and fear to something bigger and brighter. They model for all of us what it means to live a life that is authentic, powerful, generative and inspiring. I found it humbling, moving and a reminder to stay present and true to myself."

Claire Fontaine,
Author of Comeback and Have Mother, Will Travel

"Now, more than ever before, the world needs women en masse to open up their hearts, first and foremost to themselves, and then lead from there. Faces of the New Feminine Leadership brings this conversation to life by exemplifying the impact that women can make when they embrace all of who they are and share their perfectly imperfect selves with the world. Let this be the launching pad for other women to do the same!"

Liora Mendeloff,
Founder of Women Speakers Association

"The succinct message to inspire others, along with each woman's personal journey will be instrumental to our global community of women. I am very excited to help promote Faces of the New Feminine Leadership through our global community of women, and share these principles through our network. Congratulations on a wonderful book - expressing your journey to help others to be empowered. I am a huge fan!"

Tess Cacciatore,
Chief Visionary Officer of GWEN
(Global Women's Empowerment Network)
and Founder/ Executive Director of World Trust Foundation

"Faces of a New Feminine Leadership embodies the essence of female strength. Healing through community is one of the many unique strengths of the female brain. Pain shared is pain divided. By sharing these beautiful stories of vulnerability, these courageous women refuse to be victims! Instead they to stand united and victorious forging a path for anyone who dares to pass on this torch of empowerment. I saw myself in some of their stories, and I'm sure you will too."

Tana Amen, R.N., B.S.N.
New York Times Bestseller of The Omni Diet,
Vice President of the Amen Clinics

"This book touches the heart and soul of a woman's journey to her own truth and hard-earned choices to use her life and share her story to make a real difference...first by loving herself and then leading others to do the same."

Dr. Marcy Cole,
Ph.D. Holistic Psychotherapist and Founder of CMomA
(Childless Mothers Adopt) and Founder of First Tuesday

"It is so refreshing to read a book that is focused on improving yourself by focusing on your true values. Every single person needs to read Faces of the New Feminine Leadership to inspire them to reach new goals by focusing on what is truly important in life...you."

Lois Banta,
Owner/CEO Banta Consulting, Inc
and The Speaking Consulting Network

"Faces of the New Feminine Leadership is a wonderful book. It really speaks to me. It calls to me about the work I have done, and guides and shows possibilities about growth to come. For all women looking for strength and connection for their journey, this is a great read."

Brenda Berkal, DDS

"This book made me realize that we're not alone. I have felt many of the same things that were talked about in these women's stories at some point in my life. I wish that we as women could be more transparent and talk about things as we're going through them so that we could help each other and encourage each other more. Faces of the New Feminine Leadership touched my heart and made me feel like there is hope if we come together as women and share our stories of struggle and our victories!"

Heather Currie

Contents

Chapter One

Who We Are and Why Now

By Tracey Trottenberg

Who We Are and Why Now

The world is starving for feminine leadership and feminine voices. Not just from a woman in a woman's body, but feminine because of how she shows up and who she is being. When a woman is in her power, passion, radiance and joy, there is nothing more magnificent and compelling. Whether she is on a global stage or at a dinner table, as she allows herself to shine and share her truth with love and presence, the world becomes a better place. Everyone is empowered: other women, men, and children. Yet when a woman holds herself back, she holds everyone back. Other women, men, and children.

I've known this for years and have spoken this message from stages large and small. However, never before did I have as much certainty that the time for this type of feminine leadership is now: the world is ready to embrace this now more than ever, and more women yearn to speak and share their message of love, kindness and peace to create and lead change in a strategic, sustainable and spiritual way.

The women in this book are here to change the conversations in our world. Change them from fear, scarcity and competition to empowerment, abundance and community. It is time for these new conversations, now.

This is the essence of Feminine Leadership as we mean it here. The women in this book represent this type of leadership and voice. After almost twenty years immersed in the work of leading, teaching and training women in business – entrepreneurs and executives – to become feminine leaders, speakers and what we call "messengers", these are the women who have emerged as the faces of what is now and what is next.

You will experience their stories of struggle and success.

You will feel their courage and commitment to put a stake in the ground and claim a deeper truth. Taking on their own personal fears and dreams, suffering and self worth, each woman here has learned to trust herself to live and share more fully. Facing her deepest self with greater authenticity, she has given herself permission to embrace the journey to become as big as she dreams in her heart.

These are women who have been seeking to find and express their true purpose to serve and speak. They are propelled to grow themselves in consciousness and communication. These are the women who are willing to do the deep inner work while being grounded in practical spirituality and solid business strategy.

These are the *Faces of the New Feminine Leadership*. These are Amazing Women.

I feel deeply blessed to work with these women and guide them to find and express their own true voice.

Their journey is my journey too.

There was a time, nearly fifteen years ago, when I was in a previous marriage with a great man, living a beautiful life in Canada. I was traveling to the Caribbean every other month, flying first class to lead trainings, speaking at national and international conferences and coaching high-level executives. It looked like I had it all together.

On the outside, it was glamorous and great. On the inside, I was in pain. I woke up every morning feeling like I wasn't living my *real* life, as if I was caught in a trap that I said "yes" to, but I was yearning for something else.

I was ashamed and afraid, judging myself harshly and saying to myself, *I should be happy with what I have. I should love my life. What's wrong with me?* This badgering was relentless in my head; it wouldn't stop.

It was a familiar voice, one I've known my whole life. The content may have changed over the years, but the pounding of painful thoughts had been my constant companion for as long as I could remember. It pushed me to seek something different; something outside of myself that had to be better than what I felt in my private thoughts. Inside I felt broken, that I didn't matter, that I didn't really belong, and that a huge part of me was missing.

As a kid, that inner voice said, *I don't have my real father and everyone else does.* For as long as I knew - and I don't remember being told - my biological father left when I was six months old. My mom finally kicked him out late one night because she couldn't take his lying and cheating. As I grew up, I always had, and still do, an incredibly close and precious relationship with my mom. Through years of learning to understand the events of that fateful night and that time of life, my admiration for her strength and courage grew. I learned to release any resentment and instead fully recognize that it was an ultimate act of love for herself, and for me, to have him leave. I love my mother deeply and dearly, and am grateful as we continue our journey together with a beautiful love through all of life's twists and turns. And though I never saw my biological father again, the events of that night lived in my cells and left an indelible mark. The hole in my heart and fear in my system was bigger than my little body could comprehend. That body grew into a woman's body that still felt the pain of abandonment.

When I was two years old, my new dad came on the scene. We grew incredibly close and said *"we had a bond thicker than blood."* Everything looked good on the outside. Except it was terrifying on the inside.

I grew up hearing *"Tracey, you could do 10 things: 9 things right and one thing wrong, and I will always catch you do that one thing wrong."* And when I did that one thing, he would stop talking to me for days, weeks or months at a time.

It was that one thing that would set off the silent treatment, and I never knew what that one thing would be. I didn't know until I was an adult that ignoring a child is one of the worst forms of emotional and verbal abuse. It instilled in me a belief that my voice had no power and that I was not worth responding to.

I didn't know until I was an adult that this deep pain and wound would be the catalyst for my lifelong passion and purpose to transform the way we communicate to ourselves and to others: first in our own heads, then with our loved ones and then out in business and in the world.

I didn't know until I was an adult that my dad, the only dad I've known and loved, would be my greatest teacher and demonstrate both the power of pain and the power of forgiveness, as we reconciled as adults and now share a beautiful relationship. My dad did his best and passed on the generational programming he learned and experienced too. I have a world of respect for him. To me, he is walking transformation as he discovered his own path towards healing and letting go of old patterns to be more loving towards himself, and to others. I know that he loves me unconditionally, as I do him. We've shed a lot of tears, shared countless hours around the table talking, and done a lot of healing work on our own and together. I am grateful beyond words for our ongoing journey together and our soul-level contract to help each other grow and evolve.

I couldn't have known until many years later, all of the blessings that would come out of that past trauma, and that it's an old soul that creates deep childhood pain to learn about love and grow into self-actualization. To see the perfection in my own journey from a spiritual sense has become one of my greatest accomplishments for which I am so very grateful. Though I still face the demons as they arise (after all, I'm still human and have more growing to do as long as I have a pulse!), I feel great peace and deep love for myself and for all the 'players' in my life. This has come out of a relentless commitment to do my own deep inner and spiritual work, and to heal old wounds authentically.

Growing up, it was scary to never know what that moment would be that would trigger the silent treatment. I internalized the judge and jury, and they became a powerful force in my own head.

Already having lost one father, the pain and fear of losing the second one over and over again became a constant fear. Everyday I asked myself: *What's the right thing to say or do so he would talk to me?* I lived on high alert and watched for all the signs: what was said and not said, what was the energy underneath, what looks were being shot across the room, what body language was going on and so on. I could never have known that this would become a great gift of seeing and sensing all levels of communication – verbal and non – and become my life's work.

I was very sensitive to everything around me and highly intuitive. I could see, hear and feel what was spoken and unspoken. What was in the space beyond the words and what was in the energy that permeated all of it.

This intuition started to show itself during my childhood. I sensed when my grandparents were sick, when something was wrong, when we needed to avoid or do something, or when my brother needed support and protection. It was beyond anyone's understanding, and no one knew what to do with it.

This deep inner knowing came to a head at the tender age of fifteen.

At 6pm on a cold December night, we were getting ready for Friday night dinner with my family in Montreal. My beloved grandparents (on my mother's side, who helped raise me and with whom I was incredibly close) were in Florida for the winter. The voice inside me got very loud as we were sitting down at the table and I knew I needed to call my grandparents right away. It hit me suddenly and I grabbed the phone. I was told to call after dinner. Sitting at the table, I was tormented with nervous energy that coursed through my whole body: my hands were shaking, feet tapping and both my head and heart felt like I would explode from the inside. My behavior seemed crazy to those around me. Everyone around the table started casually talking about the local funeral home and I knew this was a bad topic of conversation. I could hardly swallow any food from the total anxiety in my body.

As we cleaned up from dinner, the feeling subsided and I was talking on the second phone line with a friend. The other phone rang and I immediately said "*I have to go right now*" and hung up. I looked over to my mother as she picked up the phone. She looked at me, looked at my father and said "*My mother was hit by a car.*"

I ran upstairs to be alone and wouldn't let anyone in my room. I knew it. I knew something was wrong with them. I knew something bad was happening. "*I could have saved her*" was all I kept saying to myself. I was a total mess.

I finally fell asleep. A few hours later, I woke up suddenly and sat right up, staring at the door ahead of me. Within two minutes, the phone rang and I heard my mother's muffled voice from her room. She then opened my door and sat on my bed.

My grandmother, my dear Bubby, was dead.

I already knew.

I hardly slept that night and woke to plans being made. My mother was on the first plane out and I felt a pain in my heart that I couldn't even begin to express. Others knew I was upset and anxious about making a call to Florida the night before, yet no one spoke a word of it.

The next day my mother returned, and with her was my Gramps, who was of course in shock. Just hearing his voice turned all my attention to him. He was the love of my life. My mother came in to the house first and told me he was doing OK. Yet, when he saw me, he burst out in tears. From that moment through the funeral to the week of sitting "*shiva*" (the Jewish memorial), he and I sat next to each other and held hands. All my energy was focused on him. Except for when I was sent off to study for exams.

It was devastating to have to study for exams rather than grieve and heal. As the months passed, I never truly dealt with what happened. The pain and trauma was buried inside until it blew up six months later. Sitting in class at high school, the sound of a horn honking outside triggered something in me that had me scream and sob. Sent to the principal and then to a therapist, it opened up the depth of pain and trauma from multiple abandonments: from the loss of my biological father to the many 'losses' with my father not speaking to me, to the shock of my grandmother being killed suddenly. All of this pain was brought to the surface and tied together.

Told I was a 'gifted' child in a letter by the therapist and that I was dealing with layers of abandonment, I returned back to 'normal life' and it was left at that. But for me, it was the beginning. That experience propelled me into the depth of my journey and search from therapy through transformation to teaching. I dove into my path of seeking and searching for something more. That death kicked up in me a desire and commitment to *"leave my mark."* The pain within sparked a relentless search for understanding and seeking who I was and what I'm here for. That became my everything.

As the years went on, I went from therapy to books, seminars to healers, transformational programs and retreats to finding and knowing my purpose and path to lead this work. My career grew. I started speaking and traveling, and took on leadership roles in the business community.

With all of that, I still felt alone, especially in my marriage at the time. I looked for other women with whom I could relate and figure this out. Role models who could help me through the darkness and show me how to create my life, change myself, or find some way to be happy.

I was amazed at how hard that was to find! I was tenacious and kept talking to more and more women in leadership roles and corporate positions, and many of the executive and senior-level women who were my clients at the time. I searched out other business owners, consultants and women entrepreneurs I respected or wanted to get to know and connect with at a deeper level.

I quickly found out that most of them, if not all, had similar challenges and not many answers either. I also discovered that they needed the same kind of support and craved the same conversations I was looking for. Quickly, it became obvious that if someone was going to help figure this out, it was going to be me. That's when I came to understand what has since become one of our taglines: "*You are the leader you've been looking for*™." That was me.

During those years in Canada, I started the first iteration of Amazing Women in 2002. I held events and gatherings where women would come together to talk about painful issues, unspoken dreams and vulnerable challenges. It was fabulous! I had senior-level corporate women asking profound questions about themselves, their purpose and their path that they had never before explored. At one event, a high-powered senior executive asked, "What if I'm meant to be Betty Crocker?" This question might sound mundane or even sarcastic, but it wasn't. For her, it was the first time she put down her established goals and masculine pursuit and asked her heart what it wanted. It was the first time she allowed herself to go there—to the place where there were no clear-cut answers—to find a better and deeper question she could explore. At first, she was scared to ask and reveal herself to the group, but afterwards she came over and told me how life changing that was for her.

Those moments became constant, and it was clear that this was what women needed. I hosted other events, including one in a funky downtown club where I brought in a local spiritual teacher and had thirty women in business suits rolling their hips and doing "tantric" breathing as I led a talk about femininity in business. Again, there were tears, deep questioning, and introspection. One woman, another high-powered executive, shared that she had just been diagnosed with cancer and was certain it was because she was living her life as a lie. Sobbing and witnessed by a room full of other women, she revealed that she had never said those words out loud. She blamed herself for getting sick and was terrified. With the love of the community and the support in the room as each woman gave up her game face and dropped her own mask too, she was free to see how much she was like everyone else. She was grateful, and her healing began on that very day.

I knew I was on the right track. Yet as my vision grew, so did my pain.

Even though it was obvious that I was not alone in my challenges and desires, I was still searching for something. Bringing women together was my calling, yet deep within, I felt like a fraud. I could lead and hold the conversation and transformation for others, but not yet for myself. I was unhappy in my marriage and lost within myself.

My search went on with more seminars, psychics and even people channeling spirit guides to help me know myself better. I went to a ten-day silent meditation retreat to hear my inner voice and receive direction from within, which I did. In a deep meditation, it became clear that it was time to leave my marriage and go out on my own and stop the charade. I left feeling empowered and ready to take the step I'd been so terrified to face.

Yet when I came back home and saw my caring husband, my beautiful house, and all the trappings that surrounded me, I got scared. Filled with doubt, shame and questioning myself, I became confused about what to do and panicked. My body went into a state of shock, having gone from total clarity to fear and indecision. I woke up the next morning with a horrible case of vertigo. Violently ill and in excruciating pain, I couldn't walk three feet to the bathroom. I later realized how much I betrayed myself by not following through. It took a few months before I got the courage to end the marriage, which we did in a very amicable and kind way.

This time, single and on my own, it was all about me and the inner work I knew was required. I faced many dark nights, tough moments and hard choices, yet as I stayed on my path, I kept meeting the right people at the right time in perfect divine synchronicity. After one such meeting, I headed to northern California to a retreat I knew little about but felt intuitively drawn, which catapulted my life in ways I couldn't have imagined. There I saw a photo of a spiritual teacher who was holding a retreat a few months later. I knew—just by his photo and deep penetrating eyes that I had to be there. I heard the words inside, *He's going to bust me open,* and that's exactly what I needed. I knew there would be nowhere to hide, and that's what I wanted. I was ready.

My quest was most important to me, no matter how inconvenient, where it took me or what the expense. I knew my work with women, leadership, and conscious communication was everything I was meant for and this was my path. Yet inside, I still battled the demons and critical voices of self-doubt and self-hatred.

Finding and loving myself—my authentic self and true voice —and expressing this fully were all I wanted.

13

It was that retreat and a few subsequent encounters that opened the doors to bring me to Los Angeles just over ten years ago. With nothing more than a one-way ticket, one suitcase and money for just one month's rent, I left Canada and never looked back. It was in L.A. that I knew I was meant to bring forward the deeper version of my teaching and "GodWork," as I call it. From that point on, my entire life has been about being a feminine leader, sharing my message and authentic voice, following my calling and guiding other women to do the same.

I went through many more challenges throughout the years to bring Amazing Women International, Inc. (AWI) to where it is now: immigration visas that allowed me to grow the business but left me unable to travel back to Canada for a few years. Scary cash flow dips where I had to sell my old engagement ring to pay for rent, and other ups and downs that had me often wrestling with God and on my knees in tears, praying for help.

I wouldn't trade a moment of it.

Though always a work-in-progress, I found my voice. I found my true center. I fell in love with myself authentically, and found my way to truly love the precious little girl inside of me, my inner child. I learned to trust my intuition. I transformed my inner dialogue so I could become congruent and aligned within myself and with my work in the world. I found the way to lead and guide other women to the same. I found my deeper connection with God (that's my word for my highest truth and source). And, I found my beloved soul mate, best friend and twin flame - my most amazing and gifted husband, George Peter Kansas – and together we share life and "share the stage". Today, he and I bring our collective and extraordinary work out into the world and impact thousands of lives doing what we love and living what we teach. Committed to our own spiritual evolution and growth, we still do our own deep inner work each and every day.

And now, in this book that has been waiting for the right moment to be birthed, I get to "share the stage" with these Amazing Women who are my co-authors.

We are each here with different stories, yet one message: *it's time for new conversations in our world—in business, in life, in health, in families, in feminine essence, and in leadership.*

These co-authors share the same dreams and same prayers as some of the biggest names in media, politics, and other global stages. Each woman here uses her business, her message and her life to be the example of what's possible for all of us when you do the inner work required to make a real difference on the outside. This is the only way to bring forward the much-needed conscious change, conscious communication and conscious commerce to our world.

These women represent so many others who also hunger to make this kind of impact, but aren't sure how or where to turn. These women are role models as they're figuring it out while blazing the trail.

What I've always known intuitively - but wasn't able to fully articulate because I hadn't embodied it yet - is that the world *is* starving for feminine leadership and feminine voices from women like you and me. Women willing to share their hearts and hurts. Women willing to share their brilliance and bumps. And women willing to do the work to *become* the version of herself that she dreams of in her heart, so that she can first heal and express herself, and then powerfully serve the world with her purpose.

Vulnerable and victorious, courageous and committed, this is what makes her a feminine leader.

This is what makes her Amazing.

This is what makes the women in this book get up every morning and face her day with courage and commitment to grow into her most authentic and expressed version of herself.

Willing to lead a new conversation, each woman here brings her heart, passion, joy, wisdom and her "special sauce" to share her journey and inspire you to embrace and share yours.

In order to be that kind of woman, you have to step out from the crowd and be willing to be seen. To be raw and real. Strategic and spiritual. Expansive and grounded. Willing to dig deeper to get to the heart of the matter and not step over anything. To live your message and become a "Conversation Leader™" means not making excuses or settling for the status quo.

Doing the deeper work requires the courage to go all in. To get messy in order to find your message. To embrace all of you—the fabulous and the flaws—and bring kindness to yourself. These women will show you what this journey looks like in real life.

It is a work in progress and none of us are perfect. Yet these women embody the truth of this book: it is only by going within to connect more deeply with yourself and bringing kindness, self love and self acceptance to this inner journey that you can then make a real impact 'out there' with others in your life and in the world.

It is only the woman who is willing to dig deeper...

The Dalai Lama once said, "The world will be saved by the Western Woman."

With all due and deep respect to this amazing spiritual leader, I only partially agree. I don't believe the world will be saved by the woman who is uninterested, unhealed and unwilling to do the deeper inner work required to become aware of the impact of her communication on herself and others. I believe instead, that the world will be saved by the woman who is learning to turn her pain and childhood wounds into a wand of love and leadership, while staying true to her heart and feminine qualities. A woman willing to grow and evolve the ways in which she shows up and the impact she has—verbally and nonverbally— on those in her life, business and the world at large.

The women in this book are such women. These are the *"Faces of the New Feminine Leadership."*

It's my absolute honor and delight to share with you these Amazing Women who are walking their talk and leading new conversations. Each woman embraces the change within herself and her own life first, and then brings it to her business and her work with others, whether in a boardroom, classroom, networking event, dental chair, barn, or wherever her calling and purpose take her.

Each woman leads her conversation in a way that makes a real difference: leaving people feeling better about themselves, feeling seen and heard, respected, empowered, and connected. Committed to changing the discourse of limitation and self-judgment, lack and self-doubt, each woman is becoming more aligned with her true Self. She commits daily to finding her unique voice and the way the message is uniquely delivered through her. She is not a 'talking head' that speaks from the neck up; rather her message comes from her heart and is grounded in her body. From this place, she can hold a more genuine and transformational space in which others can grow too. This is where real impact, influence and inspiration come from. This is the *new* Feminine Leadership.

This is what we do here at Amazing Women International, Inc. *Our work starts where others stop.* It is this deeper place from which true potential for real change and evolution in consciousness begins. It is where meaningful connection and transformation comes alive in conversation. It allows us to learn and reveal the unique way God (or whatever word is your expression of a higher power and truth) expresses as each one of us. It creates a stronger foundation upon which you may understand and activate your life's lessons and the unique twists and turns of your journey to be used to benefit others, and to heal yourself.

We hope you find yourself in our stories. We hope you find your story in ours. We hope you find your way to share your story too.

Let's enjoy this journey, together!

Chapter Two

Loving Myself to Lead, Ageless and Accountable

By Kristy Deegan

Kristy Deegan... An Amazing Feminine Leader

I am blessed when I meet a woman who dives in headfirst and is as steadfast in her path of transformation and personal growth as I am. Kristy is one such woman. The respect and admiration I have for her is profound. She is a woman who has lived a lot of life at her magnificent age of sixty-something, a woman who's lost a lot of love, given a lot to others, and has now found her true voice and calling as a feminine leader. She holds herself accountable beyond compare and will call you up to your highest because she cares that much. I'm grateful to be on this journey with this woman and excited for you to get to know what I know... that she is amazing and a true stand for the greatness in each and every one of us!

With love & inspiration,
Tracey

-2-
Loving Myself to Lead, Ageless and Accountable

——⸱(( )( )) ⸱——

Here I am again playing Scrabble. I know I should be writing this chapter and I just keep distracting myself. I am the queen of creative avoidance. That could be a good thing—even a funny thing—if it wasn't so painful. I feel afraid, even frantic. I feel frustrated and alone, and I am doubting myself. It's like I have to get it right and make sure it's done perfectly before I start.

So I ask myself, "Why is it that I know better, yet I still distract myself from doing what I know I should be doing?" I am attractive, intelligent, successful, and committed to service. Every endeavor I have tried has been successful and yet I feel immobilized. What's going on with me? I wonder if other people feel like this.

Let me be quiet and go inside and listen to what my inner child is saying to me. I ask her, "What are you feeling?" She says, *I am so afraid.* "What are you thinking?" *Bad things will happen if I don't get it right.*

"No, my dear, you won't be punished this time. You are loved and we'll get through this together," I reassure her.

Creative avoidance is such a convenient way to avoid feeling. Writing this book has brought up some very uncomfortable patterns and feelings. My usual MO is to recognize a pattern, assess whether it is serving me or not, and either shift it or just let it be. What I am noticing is that I don't let myself go to the deeper feelings. I gloss over them. That's why they keep coming up. The truth is one cannot really heal and move forward congruently unless one experiences and embraces the deeper feelings. Letting myself go into the pain is scary, and I reassure my little one inside that these feelings will pass. Just do it.

I am sad because I realize that I have avoided that access door to my heart. I have avoided my deepest feelings and skipped over connecting with myself—and with others and with God. Looking back, this has kept me separate and fed my feeling of not belonging. I now realize all the opportunities for connection that I missed because I held back, waited until I knew the right answer, and moved forward only if I knew I would get it right. I had to get it right or something terrible would happen to me.

I was adopted at age two years and eight months. My mom often threatened to send me back to the orphanage if I didn't do things right. I remember one time when I was about four, a lady came to visit us and had big pills that she called vitamins. My mom said I had to take them, but I couldn't swallow them. They were too big. She told me if I didn't take the pills, she would send me back to the orphanage. I tried and choked and gagged and couldn't do it. She sent me to my room. I just knew we would be going to the orphanage immediately.

This threat happened on a regular basis. When I was twelve, I got up early on Easter to find my Easter basket. There were two on the table, one for each of my brothers, but none for me. I was very sad and cried. My mom said that I was too old for Easter, and there was no basket for me. I got upset and told her she could have at least told me this. She said that I should have known. And even though I was too old for Easter, I was not too old to go back to the orphanage. I had to be perfect or I would get sent away.

Now, here's the deal. I am a very smart rat. I am sixty-eight years old. I've been around the transformational block and coached people for over twenty years, so I know how to talk the game of personal change and growth. I also know that this is a process and will show up again and again in different ways. Every time it does, I flip back and forth until the self-awareness kicks in and I make a choice. But this time I am catching my own BS, seeing the humor in my humanity, and I'm very excited about stopping this game.

Moving forward a couple years, I was living in Mexico and getting a little bored. There were only so many books I could read or sunsets to watch. I started to hear a number of horror stories about the contractors where I lived and how they handled their business dealings. Americans and Canadians would come and buy a piece of property. Then they would go home and sell their home. They would come back to Baja, give the entire cost of the house to the contractor and go back home. Rather than begin construction, the contractor, having more money than he had ever seen before, would then go buy a truck. I saw a real need here that I could help. I could serve as the foreigners' ombudsman. So, I started a construction management business.

People told me I couldn't start a business like that in Mexico; I was a woman, a foreigner, and I had no construction experience. They said I should just retire and play tennis. That wasn't an option for me. I had a vision of truly helping these people and I had to do it.

I knew nothing about building a house. Heck, I can't even throw a hammer to hang a picture. However, I knew how to manage people and projects and I could speak Spanish. So I interviewed thirty contractors and ruled out all but two. I asked a lot of questions and put up a web site for each client. In the first eighteen months of operation, the business generated over $1.7 million in revenues and set a new bar in the community for the quality of building.

Now who was I being in this scenario? Was I just looking for a way to make a buck? Or was I being the person behind the mask? Not really. I was the true me. I saw an opportunity to make life better for others. That's the heart of who I am. I am committed to serve. Plus, I had a mission. I never felt afraid or sad. I never had a moment of indecision or procrastination. It was, "Watch my dust! I don't know what I'm doing, but I'll figure it out." I had faith in me and my product, and that the Universe would make it happen. So, who was this self? I didn't hesitate, doubt, or question what I was doing. I was in total service and moving with ease and grace; it seemed so easy. Things just fell into place like magic and I was being the real me.

I know that part of me well. When I am on a purpose that is bigger than me, I soar and don't have time for small thoughts. But I also know the part inside of me that gets scared and feels stuck. Without a purpose, support, and faith I struggle.

Well, we know that the housing market fell and that affected the entire world, including my construction management business. But that didn't matter. Yes, we made less money, but I was on a mission to make life better for foreigners in Mexico. We started doing Mexican wills and providing other services that supported the gringo community. There was just something about that purpose that didn't give me time or energy to feel scared, or to hold back or have doubts. I kept going and maintained the thought in my head, "How can I solve this challenge or how can I get that done?" I loved that feeling.

Then my husband passed away of a sudden heart attack. My life changed instantly. The construction market was not coming back. Here I was, single in a resort retirement community in Mexico. I looked at the people around me and I felt so sad and misplaced. I knew I didn't belong there. Many of them acted and appeared so old—not so much in their age, but in their attitude and actions. They started drinking at 10:00 am, played dominoes every afternoon, and just seemed to be waiting for life to be done. I knew that my soul would die if I stayed in this environment. There must be more for me in this lifetime. It was time to reinvent myself.

On the tails of that high I got from being on purpose in my construction business, I made a list of all the things I wanted in my life (I wanted to be by the water, in nice weather, around people that felt alive, able to walk to shops, etc.). I searched the Internet for places that could fit the bill. During Thanksgiving and Christmas holidays of that year, I came to an area in Southern California that I loved. I drove up and down streets and found the perfect place. I went home, packed up, and moved. I believed that the Universe, God, or a Higher Power had guided me to move here. I didn't know why, but it was such a smooth transition, it must have had divine intervention.

The breakdown came a few months after I arrived and relocated to my new place. I loved where I lived and really enjoyed being back in the states. And yet there I was, yelling at people on the freeway and shaking my head. Slow ladies in the grocery line irritated me, and I wanted to hit them with my purse like Ruth Buzzi on *Laugh In*. Something was off. None of these things bothered me before. I must have been a sight, getting upset and then talking to myself to calm down. What a roller coaster. There was nothing in my life to focus me or give me more meaning. I had no purpose. Service—the heart of who I am—was nonexistent.

"How could I serve?" I asked myself. "I'll start my coaching business again," I said confidently at that moment. "I already have a track record of getting amazing results with people and businesses. I created a multimillion-dollar business in a foreign country in a man's world. Yes, I can do this!"

Networking seemed like a good way to meet people, but I had never officially done that before. My clients all came by word of mouth. I quickly realized that it is difficult to create a roster of tons of new clients and a thriving business when I know only six people. The problem was, I found networking very shallow. How could I cram more than thirty-five years of business and personal experience into a one-minute commercial? "What a crazy idea!" I thought to myself, and the self-doubt hit again. But others seem to get business this way. "I must be obsolete," I thought. That inner voice of fear and doubt became very strong. "I'll just be positive and keep going." (See how I continued to step over connecting with myself and experiencing the deeper feelings?)

My website and networking groups were not getting me referrals. "How can I get people to go to my website? How can I get referrals?" I asked myself these questions over and over. I put on my customer hat and got strategic. "As a customer I would not hire someone right off an Internet web page, nor would I refer someone to an unknown person." My potential clients had to connect and resonate with *me*, not a website. I quickly realized the website was only a tool, an adjunct to the avenue of success. Networking is a long-term process to help people know, like, and trust me. Though my inner strategist was onto something, my doubts also crept in: "I must be obsolete," I thought, but then I countered, "I'll show you. I can do it, too." And again, dove in feet first.

But something was still missing inside me, even though I did what I had to do and it was working. The business was growing, but it was all on top of a disempowered thought. I just kept driving forward on top of a fear inside of feeling obsolete. Any good thing I accomplished, any client I got, any success I experienced was all on top of this belief and fear, so it never felt truly satisfying or authentic.

The smart rat was in full bloom but I couldn't distract myself from what I was really feeling deep down. No matter what success and good I experienced, inside I couldn't really accept, appreciate, or love my real self. I was almost forlorn. On I went, but it was hard and a lot of work. It was not the effortlessness I had known when I was on a mission in Mexico in my construction business.

Then I "accidentally" got a new client. She was assigned to evaluate me to see if I would fit with a specific networking group. We hit it off, she hired me, we worked splendidly together, and she soared. We attended a fundraiser together and another lady at the table said to her, "You look fabulous. What's changed?" My client said, "I have a coach." Voila! I enrolled a second client. Accidents? But that inner voice was still loud. I wouldn't admit to myself that I wasn't obsolete, even with clients coming after me. It was like I had one foot in and one foot out.

Then I found another way to "creatively avoid" jumping in fully with my coaching business, and the smart rat was back in action: I had a bad knee and needed a knee replacement. "Why, I couldn't get work with new clients and then be out of commission in the middle. Better not to start." Can you believe it? That smart rat is good! She is sneaky and very convincing, and even with things going well, I was still in creative avoidance and not accessing the deeper parts of myself that wanted my attention. Even with all the positives, it seemed easier to walk away or avoid what I was I feeling deep inside. Somehow the pain of going in seems worse than the pain of NOT going in. I can't imagine why that is. And, once again I feel miserable and full of self-doubt.

I knew I needed a coach/mentor in order for me to get out of my own way and manage my internal conversations, but I needed someone smarter than my smart rat! I interviewed several and couldn't find one that I knew would hold me to the path of my highest self. I told myself that I was a better coach than many of them. After all, as smart rat I could run circles around them. I could not find one that I truly resonated with. However, I also knew that my self growth is my responsibility, not the coach's. So I kept looking. I knew that my peace of mind and well-being depended on finding a coach and mentor to lead me from my agony and get back on purpose. Finally, I found Tracey Trottenberg. She could see me, like I could see my clients behind their masks. She could manage and work with smart rats like me and hold me to account. And she was so spiritual and loving that I knew she was for me.

Through working with a mentor and diving even deeper into myself, I have discovered that I am not obsolete. I couldn't be. I am sixty-eight years old. I have been around the block—in business and in my personal life. I bring wisdom beyond expectation and look at what I know, what I've done, and my commitment to growing. Owning this is so freeing. I am a messenger with a purpose. That's actually why I am writing this chapter. I know there are a lot of you out there who experience the pain of feeling unneeded, unwanted, and obsolete; who experience the pain of needing to get it right before you make a move. I really know what that feels like.

I've learned that so much of what we tell ourselves is a lie, even though that inner voice of doubt and fear feels so real. I know that I have a choice, a purpose, and I can connect with God to deliver on that purpose. The same is true for other women like me, maybe a woman like you. There is no magic bullet, no magic destination. There is no arrival to a place where there is no more pain. The pain is our teacher and helps us see where we are being a "smart rat" and holding back instead of going within. This is a life process. It will never end, AND you can manage it with ease and grace.

Boy, did my stuff come up again when I took on this project of writing a chapter in this book. Even though I had gone deeply into myself and healed so much, the smart rat found a new "cheese" with this one. Before I knew it (literally, before the smart rat was in full swing), I found myself in deep creative avoidance. This time it was Scrabble! You wouldn't believe how many Scrabble games I've played in the few weeks before I began writing. I would get scared and play Scrabble to avoid and numb myself so that I didn't have to write. Even with all the work I've done on myself, those old internal conversations came back. I would start to feel sadness or anxiety that I wouldn't "get it right" or be clear about my message, so I would skip right to playing

Scrabble. Or I'd get a snack or read a magazine. But this time was very different: I laughed as I saw that old smart rat again. I knew that I needed to go through the door to my deepest heart to access the old pain and experience it, so I could let it go and stay true to my purpose. In the past, I would have come right up to that door and turned away as I did many times. Now, the real "smart me" opened it and walked right in.

Though I saw the pain and sadness, I could see the all the good too. Every time I experience pain, there is a lesson to learn and a joy to feel as I come out on the other end a better self. And this time I could laugh at the "dance" of the back and forth.

I've come to learn that this dance is the ego self, and it never totally goes away. In fact, it gets sneakier, smarter, and more rat-like, always looking for that piece of cheese. The key is to recognize that it is showing up and shift to what's in my heart and my true self. So this time I dove in even more to connect with myself and be with my pain— my fear of not getting it right. In the past, I lived with constant fear that "something bad would happen if I didn't get it right." As a little girl that was true. In this season of my life, I know that the only truth is that I'm okay.

I used to go right up to the doorway to intimacy and walk away, using some creative way to avoid and just shift my thinking. Now I go in, and I ask myself with no judgment attached, "Why did I manifest this experience, accident, joke, whatever? What am I trying to avoid? What am I not wanting to be with?" I look to see what feeling is there. It's usually some sense of inadequacy, needing to get it right, or needing to look good. I have found that when I allow myself to go through the door and experience the underlying feelings, I find gold on the other side. The power of the feelings subsides, and I can jump into what I have been avoiding. I discovered that I am the creator of my life and experiences. And I find peace and joy to be connected.

That's not to say that the fear never shows up. The ego self is always on the lookout for ways to manifest. That smart rat is always hungry! My true self must continuously check to see if we are aligned. There are no accidents or coincidences. If I drop something, make a joke, trip, show up late, anything at all, I look to see what I am avoiding (How am I being that THAT shows up? I keep myself on a very short leash.). The rewards are so wonderful that I continue without any reservation.

When I live on purpose and allow God to work through me, miracles happen. I allow God to use me for coaching people through the process of going through that door to their pain and coming out on the other side, feeling free and believing that they are not and never could be obsolete. I allow God to use me to teach people that they are here for a purpose, what that purpose is, and how to stay aligned with it no matter what. I have a mentor to hold me to my highest. We are not alone and we shouldn't try to do it alone. Having a purpose can alter your inner conversation from needing to get it right to "watch my dust—this will be." That is so powerful.

Key takeaways...

- Access the door to your heart: the doorway to intimacy. Experience your pain and suffering and open the door to peace, joy, and freedom. We must heal ourselves first so that we may lead others.

- Our thoughts never stop. We can choose to listen to the disempowering ones or choose to stay on the path of purpose. You have a choice, moment by moment, to stay on purpose. You can shift anytime you want.

- There are no accidents. Pay attention to when you tell jokes, cut yourself off, or check out of a conversation. These are messages from the universe to stop, look, and learn. Who are you being that you created this?

- Get a mentor. When you do it alone, you are only rearranging your own opinions and judgments. A neutral, trained third party committed to your success can lead you to your success.

About the Author, Kristy Deegan

Kristy Deegan has been coaching individuals and businesses since 1991. She holds a bachelor's degree in nursing and a master's degree in management. She has created a life she loves, and it's her goal to empower as many people as she can to do the same for themselves. You can reach life-changing clarity through transformational and permanent shifts in your perspective. You can produce breakthrough results in predetermined areas. You participate in the custom designing of your process for growth with a clear path for action and milestones for the measurement of your success. AND we will laugh our way to your success.

Kristy Deegan has extensive experience in psychiatric nursing, sales, marketing, computer installation, and management consulting. She achieved the number one salesperson position for three separate organizations. Kristy has owned three businesses, including a construction management company in Mexico that generated revenues of $1.7 million within eighteen months. The businesses have prospered and flourished by implementing the very same foundational work she uses for her clients today. She brings business expertise to the table and wisdom in personal development to assist you in attaining your desired success. You have what it takes.

She brings the inquiry and expanded awareness that opens your evolution, identifies your purpose, and puts you in action. She offers individual and group coaching, accountability process, teleconferences, and is a sought-after speaker to small and large groups on topics such as personal development/leadership, accountability, and growing your business.

Can you imagine a life that brings you ultimate joy, pleasure, and fulfillment that you can measure and a life that you love? Can you picture your business soaring with ease and grace?

Go to Kristy's website and get started with your free "5 Secrets to Soul Level Results". Or find her on Facebook.

She looks forward to meeting you!

A Personal Message from Kristy Deegan

https://youtu.be/WiZDvVFOYhc

http://www.kristydeegan.
com/5secretsforsoullevelresults

From Kristy - What it means for me to be a Face of the New Feminine Leadership

Sharing my story so that others can get in touch with their feminine side is an honor and a responsibility. A feminine leader leads from the heart and has the courage to stand for others greatness no matter what. As a feminine leader I continue to do my own inner work so that I can stay connected to myself, Community and God so I can be that stand.

Connect with Kristy Deegan

You can find out more about Kristy Deegan and connect with her directly here:

Email: kristy@kristydeegan.com

Website: www.kristydeegan.com

Twitter: www.twitter.com/kristydeegan

Facebook: facebook.com/kkdeegan

Linked In: www.linkedin.com/kristydeegan

Blog: www.kristydeegan.com/kristy-deegan-blog.html

Chapter Three

Why I Am Alive

By Lisa Margulies

Lisa Margulies... An Amazing Feminine Leader

When two souls collide and come together in absolute knowing and familiarity, it's magnificent. It was George, my husband, who first connected with Lisa and knew in his heart that she and I needed to know each other. Within an instant of meeting, Lisa and I recognized our soul-level connection, and that we were meant to work and walk this path together. There is nothing "halfway" about her: she is all in with her heart, soul, purpose, and brilliance. She is a feminine leader that is helping to transform lives and bring a new context to the financial conversation on our planet. I'm thrilled to share this amazing woman who will knock you on your heels and help you stand upright again ... just a little shock, awe, and grounded goodness.

With love & inspiration,
Tracey

-3-

Why I Am Alive

Have you ever felt like you lived the hardest life ever? Have you ever just wanted to give up and die? Have you ever asked yourself, "What is the freakin' point to all of this? NOTHING makes any sense!" Well, I have. I grew up in hell. Actually, somewhere in the 1980s I made up a word ... "heinosity." My life was a heinosity. I was shocked when I Googled it for kicks recently to see that it was an entry in the Urban Dictionary. Apparently, I am not the only one who has felt like this.

A few years ago I watched the movie *Precious* that was produced by Oprah Winfrey. My childhood was kind of like that, except it was set in a rural farming community, my perpetrator was my grandfather, the psycho was my mother, and my dad was a loving beater.

I became bulimic when I was ten and progressed into anorexia later into my teens. I remained anorexic and bulimic for nineteen years until I got pregnant with my first child at age twenty-nine. I spent middle school and high school disassociated, floating from classroom to classroom on the ceiling, watching myself in third person. We were poor, but boy were we Born Again. Things that were done to me as a kid in the name of Jesus should be criminal ... oh, right, they are.

One of the many highlights of my teenage life was that I had volunteered to work in a center-city mission. The mission director was a marvelous, Born Again Christian black man named Leon. I thought it would be nice to invite him to have dinner with our Born Again Christian family. I would never have guessed that would result in my dad pointing a gun at me, holding me hostage in my bedroom, and then threatening to kill Leon, me, and then himself. That was when I completely understood the family story of when my grandmother told my dad about when she found him with the love of his life and she happened to be a Native American.

She said, "There will be no papooses in my house! The redbirds and the bluebirds don't mix!" The interesting thing was that my grandmother was a quarter Cherokee. Christianity and racial discrimination seemed to go hand in hand. Love was so strangely defined for me by my environment. Somehow, after hours of me stubbornly holding on to my belief that Christians were Christians and that it had nothing to do with color, he lost his nerve and let me go. I did not speak to him for over two years after that.

I wanted to die so badly and life would not let me. My dad was a hunter-gatherer type. I was the oldest, and it was well known that he cried when I was born because I was not a boy. That did not stop him from taking me out hunting and fishing as though I were a boy. He lost me in the woods during a blizzard one deer season. It was nothing short of a miracle that he found me as I was freezing to death and about to walk down a godforsaken, treacherous part of the back side of the mountain as I had become disoriented and lost.

I could not commit suicide because it would be a sin, so I fantasized about the relief I would feel if a baseball bat cracked my head open and sprayed my brains on the wall. I even liked visualizing the blood spatter patterns and thought it looked like art. My life was surreal. That is all I can say.

The physical abuse showered upon me by the men in my family, in the end, was not my undoing. It was my mother's mental, emotional, and spiritual abuse. I now suspect that she has an undiagnosed dissociative identity disorder with bipolar disorder. The stories I can tell would make an award-winning novel and movie, too. I was a good girl—I mean a really good girl. I guess since I was the firstborn, they truly believed in Original Sin. Add into that a mother who had been in thirteen different foster homes, molested by her alcoholic stepdad, and treated like shit by her alcoholic mom, my home life was a force of nature. Her real father was so drunk one night that when his car stopped and he went to check under the hood, he passed out and died by searing himself to the engine. How many have that as a family story?

I was not allowed to go to regular college like other kids because I was "so bad." I had to go to Bible college. I made it through two and a quarter years of that nightmare before enrolling myself in community college. I was so dysfunctional by that time. It hurts to remember what it took to get straight A's, which I did, yet I had to leave because I was penniless and unable to support myself. As a frame of reference, you should know that I ran away from my home in Pennsylvania and ended up in Santa Monica, California, where I went to community college. I was disowned and cut off from everything and everyone for the first time ... but there were several other times, and I will share that as they occur. I ended up in Pacific Palisades living with and caring for a ninety-year-old woman in exchange for housing. Her daughter-in-law was so nice and loving, but her son was a mean SOB. I thought moving to LA would get me away from physical abuse, but witnessing a man in his sixties strike and push his ninety-year-old mother nearly put me over the edge. The lovely daughter-in-law introduced me to her alcoholic son and his girlfriend; they in turn introduced me to a man who drugged and raped me three times.

I knew I needed to die. This Earth was not worth living on. However, I kept on living. Nothing seemed to take me out. I woke up every morning with air still in my lungs after begging God at night to please take me. I guess I don't have to tell you that this is the "cliff notes" version. The myriad of stories between these few lines makes me cry as I type this.

Eventually, I managed to enroll in the extension program at UCLA and earn my certificate as a paralegal. That is when I got the call. I was no longer disowned and I should come home. I should have run in front of a bus, but I didn't. I went back to Pennsylvania with my new paralegal certificate from UCLA and thought that I could at least get a job. I drew in a hated breath, packed my car with a few belongings, and drove back to the Heinous Hell I had run from. Going back was crazy. Let's just say things did not end well. I was disowned again and so I had to leave after three months.

The East Coast snobbery surprised me. Philadelphia had a paralegal school, and my certificate from UCLA was worthless. I finally begged my way into a job for an estate planning and tax law firm in central Philadelphia. At this firm, I had the "pleasure" of working for a partner who had a brain tumor that caused his personality to change. He was awful but I needed the job. On July 1, 1984, I moved into an efficiency apartment in a little town south of Philadelphia. It was pouring rain outside, and once I had my stuff moved in, my eyes, heart, and soul poured rainy tears even harder than the rain outside.

At some point, the outside rain stopped, and I could hear amazed voices outside my sliding glass door that had a tiny balcony. I went out to see that a perfect double rainbow had formed over my building. There was a woman named Susan standing two balconies away, and she and I got to talking. She was the lead singer in a band, and after a couple hours of talking, she said, "Boy, do I have the man for you."

Susan set me up on a blind date, and that is how I met my husband. He was in law school at the time. His mom was so wonderful and loving. She was Jewish, but she was the most Christian person I had ever met. Because of her, I eventually decided to convert to Judaism and began a spiritual journey into Kabbalah and then into Qabalah.

Remember the partner at the law firm who had the brain tumor? Well, his partner was the cantor at the largest conservative synagogue in Philadelphia. One evening, this gentleman comes into my office, closes the door, and asks me if I am dating a Jewish boy. He was furious and called me a *shiksa*. I did not know what it was, but his tone of voice let me know whatever it was, it was not good. I was in shock. I could not believe the hatred and discrimination being heaped on me. I went home and asked my boyfriend's mother about it. She was so comforting and reassured me that all was okay. I knew I was in the right place. As things progressed over the next couple years and I was to marry, I was finally and permanently disowned. Not only was I marrying out of the faith, but my mother considered Jews to be equal to blacks, and my sentence was ostracism. My mother has never met my children. My father and I reconciled somewhat many years later at the goading of his new wife and my children did get to meet him a couple of times. He passed away in June 2009.

As a paralegal, it was my job to write new pension and profit-sharing plan documents from the IRS code and regulations from scratch. I hated it, but I did it flawlessly and received IRS approvals. It was during this time that I discovered my love of accounting and math. I was really good at it. After that year, I decided to go to an administration-only firm, get out of the law business, and focus on the compliance, investments, and accounting aspects. After my soon-to-be husband graduated from law school, we relocated back to Los Angeles where he got a job in a Santa Monica–based law firm. It was actually a fairly good time in my life. I focused on becoming an expert in ERISA (pension) plan design and administration. It was a time when investment firms were looking to buy administration firms, so I started my own third-party administrative firm and consulted other firms. I aided them through their mergers, all the while perfecting my practice in compliance and accounting. I built a client base in excess of 250 clients with $100 million in assets that I maintained for twelve years. I was still anorexic and bulimic, but life was not as bad as it had been. I could focus on something that was a personal accomplishment.

Our first child was born in 1991. He was a wonderful baby. Our second child was born in 1994, and she was also a wonderful baby. Both births were Cesarean sections, but the second had gone horribly wrong. I descended back into hell. I ended up bleeding for two years, after which I contracted adult chicken pox. The virus raged through my body over a six-week period, ending in a massive hemorrhage. I ended up with an emergency hysterectomy. At some point during the initial hemorrhage and before I had the hysterectomy, I had a most profound and life-changing near-death experience. I was released from the hospital to begin my recovery; however, I did not get better. In fact, I got sicker and sicker. I was constantly, violently sick with flu-like symptoms, and my entire body was racked with pain. It took about a year before they figured out that the virus had destroyed my immune system.

To complicate matters, my four-year-old son became very difficult. At first, I thought it was because of the new baby, but one day he came to me crying with a string in his hand and wrapped around his throat in an attempt to kill himself. My return into the surreal was instant. I was so sick, and now my son was distressed. Between my bad days, I took to finding help for him. I was fortunate to be directed to an educational psychologist who performed many tests. It was determined that he was a genius with two different processing disorders. He had a visual processing and perception disorder and an auditory processing and perception disorder. At his young age, what that meant was he could understand way more than most kids, but he could not express it. The diagnosis came with the prognosis that, at that time, 90 percent of these kids killed themselves before age nineteen. I made the decision that my child was going to be in the 10 percent. Because of that decision, he became my teacher.

The next five years are hard to describe. It is where I lost it all and found it all. I am so grateful to my doctors. I had a medical doctor who was also trained in Eastern medicine and homeopathy. His wife was a Jungian psychologist, and his daughter was also a PhD candidate in psychology; all of them were gifted energy workers and spiritually awakened. I attribute who I am today to the work they did over those five years. Remember when I was saying I wanted to die? Well, I did for a few minutes. Even then, I didn't remain dead. I am meant to be alive. I have a purpose.

Because of being sick, I had to sell my third-party administration/pension servicing company. I could not manage it in my condition. Thus began a time in bed, being quiet, and seeking answers internally. I pursued my spirituality and allowed my interests to cover any and every topic. It was intellectually, emotionally, and psychologically a very quiet, regenerative soul time. As I mentioned previously, my near-death experience was profound and life changing. I will share a bit of that experience shortly. It was a turning point in my life.

At the end of five years, I was tired. We were nearly bankrupt from medical bills. My marriage was dead, and since I had no fear of death, I felt it was time to "go home." I had this quietness settle over me as I knew the fight to survive had ended. I decided to stop eating and stop taking the medications I was on, which by then covered most of a coffee table. The Master Cleanse fast was popular, so I decided I would use that as my fasting and passing. I stopped showing up for my doctor appointments. I started cleaning up my house as best as I could; hunger was not even a problem, for the decision was so complete.

Surrender ... to me, surrender is peaceful, like my near-death experience. Letting go of strife is a very peaceful process for me. The sense of freedom that I found in the letting go of everything material and preparing myself to die was truly magnificent. I did not have that luxury prior to my near-death experience; that was sudden, violent, and forced on me. This time, for me, coming to a sense of completion was profoundly powerful. As I prepared to die, my mental state developed crystal clarity. I was clear about what things were important to me. My heart took over and dictated where my mind went. (Vesting my life in heart choices is how I now live.) During this period, my heart took me on an inner journey that ended forty days later in a complete healing. I discovered that my heart directed my mind to a healing process that allowed me to truly own the idea that disease comes from dis-ease. As I allowed myself and my Self free rein to investigate subjects like how a virus replicates, how cells breathe, and how neurons connect, I discovered that I contained within me all that I needed to heal. My near-death experience and this forty-day fast would make two separate books within themselves.

I love living. To me, life is so precious. Every breath I breathe is breathed with gratitude. Every pair of eyes that I get to meet with mine is my daily blessing. I bring eyes up here because I wanted to share a small bit of my near-death experience as it profoundly influences me daily. My experience is quite long and detailed; however, to orient you, I transitioned from my body to a white room where I was surrounded by many individuals. Some were my advisors, guardians, etc., and others were there to observe what I was about to do. My advisors presented me with a series of choices. The first choice was did I want to come back, and my answer was an immediate "yes." I was then presented with four "maps." Each map was like a topographical relief map. It had a starting point that related to a health condition I would have when I re-entered my body. Each map also had an endpoint that was referenced as a goal or a purpose that, when completed, meant that I would be able to die complete.

When my eyes rested on the fourth map, I knew it was my true heart's desire. It was the most beautiful thing I had ever seen. As I was taking in the beauty of the map, I realized that it was filled with lights. It was something. It made my heart open and burn in love. The other maps were removed, and that one was centered in front of me. Suddenly there was frenetic activity. I witnessed beings running in and out of the room at what appeared to be lightning speed. It took a while for me to understand what was happening, and slowly it dawned on me that agreements were being made. I realized that each light on the map represented a person I was to meet.

After recovering, I got a job working for Washington Mutual Bank. I worked with the public, helping them with their accounts and finance-related issues, questions, and concerns. It was there that I realized that every person I met *agreed* to meet me. From then on, I have looked forward to meeting people so that I can see what gift we agreed to exchange. I have lived this way ever since. It is such a free and beautiful way to live.

What does all of this have to do with being a financial advisor? Well, in a word, everything. Being a financial advisor is sacred to me. I am afforded the blessing of being made privy to the depths of individual and family experiences that others may not have the privilege of experiencing. I look at my position as one of being a fiduciary. The law says I am a fiduciary, but truly the legal definition pales to mine. My life was a scary life. Fear seems to rule the media outlets. As I stated earlier, I worked for Washington Mutual Bank as it was failing during the financial crisis, and I saw fear in clients' eyes like no other time. It was then that I realized that all I had lived through was my strength and courage. I realized that I had moved from victim to victor, and in doing that, I created a "bank of courage and strength."

I learned to allow my clients to borrow my excess strength and courage when they could not find their own. As I looked into their eyes, I knew we had agreed to meet and the gift I could offer them was the lesson of my full life. While other advisors' practices diminished, mine grew. As my practice grew, I became bolder in being responsible for creating the safe space necessary for clients to open their hearts, be vulnerable, and discover their visions. This included their family dynamic and all their preconceived notions, regardless of whether it was about money, family, news, religion, or life in general. It included their mortality and the mortality of those they loved. It included everything in the media and news about how horrible things are in our world today. I was surprised to discover that within all my own stories of pain were others' stories. I opened a space for others to be vulnerable and share heartbreak about family disputes. I listened to how others had felt isolated, alone, and unloved. I supported individuals as they faced their own deaths due to a terminal condition and helped them prepare. I always had tissues at my desk and shared tears equally with laughs. Here I grew in the wealth of connection and so did they.

Up until that time, I craved connection and desired to be understood more than anything. Life was not worth living without it. Now, I see myself as a "fiduciary of connection." Money is meaningless without connection. I have sat with clients who had more money than they could ever spend, and they confided in me their desire to die. Their family was broken or gone. They felt alone and unloved. They came to me because caring for their money was a "to do." What they really wanted was "to be." Seeing myself as a fiduciary of connection, I allow myself to take a stand for their life and for my own. I see my own pain in theirs and can meet them where they are ... where I was and perhaps, in small part, still am. Here is the starting place. Here is where a plan can formulate. Here is where purpose becomes clear. Having a clear purpose makes life worth living, and in its completion, it makes moving on from this life so much easier.

In 2012, sixty-seven death certificates passed over my desk at the branch of the bank where I was working. My long tenure at the branch allowed me to get to know so many individuals and families. The number of families that I assisted through the grief and planning process was, to me, like attaining the equivalent of an Ivy League degree in financial planning that year. I do not think I would have been able to do it had I not gone through my own near death and then through my own planning to die. I am lucky.

The combination of my own personal life experiences and those I have shared with my clients is not easily duplicated. One death in particular touched me deeply. A client's ninety-four-year-old mother had come home to receive end-of-life hospice care there. There were last-minute changes to the trust. I was invited over to their home so that the daughter did not have to leave her mother's side. As I connected with her mother's eyes and held her hand, I knew that I was doing exactly what I was meant to be doing. I lived so that I could serve in this way. I can walk with others along life's path anywhere it goes as I have walked it myself. Trusting that I am carried by divine purpose allows me to create the same safe feeling for others.

As a financial advisor dealing with money, I must pause and say that financial literacy does include knowledge. There is a woeful lack of it.

The pain of ignorance in money matters right now is like no other time in our history. I see it as a side effect of our own lack of connection. We have lost our way to connect within ourselves and with each other. It is my purpose to reconnect what got disconnected. I have made it my purpose to give to every person I meet the time it takes to give them a gift of something they did not know about themselves and chance to see themselves differently than before they met me. I am committed to opening a new space for new possibilities for them within them. If they are financially literate, I offer my affirmation and share a moment to celebrate their success and to encourage them to share their knowledge with others.

With all that I've lived and now seen with my clients, I have a special place in my heart for the aging process. It really wasn't until I began writing this chapter that I realized the impact my first experiences in California had on me. I lived with a wealthy family. Witnessing that sweet old mother's son hit and push her has stayed with me all these years. The other understanding that is opening up for me as I write this has to do with protection. I have experienced deeply what it means to be unprotected. I think it is natural that I am in a role of protector. It is very different from what I thought it would be. Growing up in the hunter-gatherer farming environment, protecting was always couched in a warlike manner that included guns and religion. Being right about something entitles one to be violent.

What I have learned through my own life experiences is that being right ends up with me being alone and unprotected, while being empowered ends up with me connected and protected. As I experimented with becoming empowered within myself, I grew in my ability to connect more deeply, and I distanced myself from being right and isolated. As a fiduciary of connection, I find that the safe space that I create is the very thing I protect. Keeping safe space a priority allows me to facilitate my clients in remaining in their center and empowered no matter how challenging the conversation about money is. Their eyes and focus remain on what they are envisioning, and I assist them in achieving their goals. I protect them from their own inner fears, outside influences and negative thinking that distracts and drains energy (money) away from their vision and commitments.

I admit, though, I do have visions of turning over the moneychanger's tables when it comes to finances. Elizabeth Warren, a US Senator from Massachusetts, is taking a stand for "We, the people." If I were to stand up, I would speak to the power of being connected. It is in being disconnected from our own selves and each other that we are finding ourselves powerless and under the influence of media and political fearmongering. I contribute my daily practice of living a connected, empowered life and creating it one-on-one as my civic contribution. Perhaps my vision is that one day, I will be able to do it on a greater scale and support a movement that is connected and abundant for all.

The Golden Pearl

By Lisa Margulies – 10/18/2002

Oh, Wretched Heart wracked with pain,
I return to Loveless life again.

Oh Tortured Heart pierced through the core,
Why must I again endure?

Was not once, twice or thrice enough?
Blood runs warm from base of gruff.

How low must one go
To reach the heights of down below?

How high must one fly
To touch the bottom of the sky?

Broken hearts and broken wings
These are a few of my favorite things.

Lessons of Love are hard to learn.
The lesson lies in being spurned.

Wretched nights never dawn to day
The gloom sinks always in the same way.

Shadows cast long images in a row
Of things my heart has been subject to blow.

Down, down into the murky swirl
Once again I surrender to find the Golden Pearl.

I wrote this poem just after I had gotten well and a couple weeks before my husband left me. Because of my life experiences, I am blessed with words. Being able to articulate, reframe, and rephrase is a very empowering tool. I look back on all that I have been through, and I see that I have collected a treasure house of Golden Pearls. Managing the wealth of money is unequaled next to managing the wealth of experience. As a financial advisor, I get to do both.

In closing, I would like to comment briefly on family dynamics. As I have shared, family can be our greatest pain and also our greatest resource. Day after day, so many individuals and families sit before me with the weight of the world and burden of family on their shoulders. I can definitely relate to the weight of these issues. I would never want my children to go through what I went through. As a mother, I have diligently attempted to raise my children in a loving environment. Being blessed with a special-needs son and all that goes with it, including sibling rivalry, surviving divorce, and living life has softened my heart. In the world of finance, family dynamics are always at the heart of our decisions. My son and daughter have taught me more than any other teacher I have encountered. They have provided me an opportunity to risk being vulnerable, forgo judgment, and listen with an open heart to hear what they are saying under their words and "go there." Supporting them to have the life of their dreams is my greatest calling.

My son gave me the opportunity to opt out of medication, which caused me to commit to talking everything out. I will never forget when his ten- and eleven-year-old friends came to me and asked my why he was so "emo." I did not even know what that meant. They explained that it was being angry, frustrated, emotional, and moody. Since he struggled with deep depression, I took the opportunity to be very honest and trust these young kids with sensitive truths about him. He has these same friends today. The courage to be honest and trusting in that situation has yielded dividends beyond my comprehension. They taught me to recognize loving intention, foster it, and create safe space where surviving against the odds is possible. Being vulnerable allowed me the ability to create a supportive community. You may say, "Well, they are children."

These children have been there when my son needed help. There have been multiple times when I received emergency calls from him saying he was going to give up. I have had to swallow my heart and borrow courage to drive to wherever he was to talk and to allow him to choose life. We talked through everything, and it did not matter how long it took. This is an inflated situation that truly exists on a smaller scale within each of us. Bottom line, there is a scared child inside each one of us asking for help, a child who needs the time to express itself so a new choice of a vision of hope can be made.

I see the loving child in all of us. Pure hearts exist. When I close my eyes, I can feel my own—that is how I know it exists in all of us. I have learned to see the pure-hearted inner child in all I encounter. It is humbling and fills me with gratitude every time I receive a response from that place in another. There is so much being spoken about the psychology of money and the dignity of growing older. I have found that there is a timeless place within each of us that, when touched, creates miracles. I witness miracles daily.

There are very few courses, certifications, or licenses that touch on this. I treasure the gifts of others who brought themselves and their lives to my desk and showed the patience and commitment to the process of creating a successful plan. It is easy to learn the mechanics of money. The energy behind money is irresistible. I have seen perfect mechanics fail because the person's energy was invested in something else. They knew the structure was correct, but their vision was not aligned. There is very little point in creating a plan that does not align with an individual's truths and goals. Discover your truth that underlies the goal, and then the plan will naturally come up to support it.

In my opinion, a financial advisor helps you integrate both. If I could give any advice, it would be to interview many potential advisors. You will "recognize" your advisor. They will inspire you to be in a committed relationship with yourself first and your money second. You will know in the depth of your being that they are there for you and not the other way around. Valuing yourself first will help you discover the financial advisor who will become your trusted team member. We all have the right to be students and to learn from great teachers. There is great strength in humility. Feelings of shame leave us powerless and disconnected. The ability to humbly say, "I need help" and have a financial professional respect it as the beautiful offering it is will create a wealthy relationship that supports you in creating and maintaining monetary wealth. You have the right to be wealthy both on the inside and out.

As a financial advisor, it is assumed that I am limited to monetary wealth management. I am not. I know that it takes only one small shift and a fortune can be made. I extol conscious business practices as opportunities to support each other in reaching our highest potential. This is a profitable and abundant mindset. Eliminate fear-based thinking, and scarcity and poverty will disappear. What is left is abundance. My children have taught me to reach out and ask for support. They have taught me to be connected. In being connected, I have found strength and courage where I thought none existed. I lost everything and have rebuilt from nothing. My son is twenty-four, and my daughter is twenty. These past two decades have been the best training grounds money can buy. I will never be convinced that a diploma is better than experience, although I am committed to having my children get theirs. Turning inward and connecting to my inner teacher first allows me to hear differently when I listen to all the information "out there." Being rich in wisdom from the fire of experience is what I get to offer others. My gold is non-monetary; however, I understand the parallels that exist in money. I have discovered that how we handle money is the side effect of our life experience. The value of being reflective and connected internally is the secret to being connected to the wealth we desire to create and maintain. To me, maintaining both the need to be right and a know-it-all attitude is scarce and weak. Having a vast network and the ability to say, "I don't know—let me find out" have allowed me to be authentic. In the end, connection is rooted in authenticity. I feel great when someone allows me to be my most authentic, congruent, and virtuous self. I pay it forward by allowing others the same space. It is why I am alive.

Key takeaways...

- I have learned to embrace all of me. I am committed to being fully connected to my pure-hearted inner child. She is wise beyond my years and a great teacher. Being connected with her allows me to see that every challenge I overcame is my gold.

- I have discovered that how we handle money is the side effect of our life experience. The value of being reflective and connected internally is the secret to being connected to the wealth we desire to create and maintain. I believe I have the right to be wealthy, both on the inside and out. I value my experience, and I hope that my story will help you value yours, too.

- Interview many potential advisors. You will "recognize" your advisor. They will inspire you to be in a committed relationship with yourself first and your money second. You will know in the depth of your being that they are there for you and not the other way around. Valuing yourself first will help you discover the financial advisor who will become your trusted team member.

- We all have the right to be students and to learn from great teachers. There is great strength in humility. Feelings of shame leave us powerless and disconnected. The ability to humbly say, "I need help" and have a financial professional respect it as the beautiful offering it is will create a wealthy relationship that supports you in creating and maintaining monetary wealth. You have the right to be wealthy both on the inside and out.

About the Author, Lisa Margulies

———— ⟶ (( )( )) ⟵ ————

Lisa joined Regatta Capital Group, LLC in November 2014, after her tenure with JP Morgan Securities LLC as a private client advisor in a retail banking location serving the Westchester community. Her practice included helping extended client families in five states. Lisa has a powerful sense of financial stewardship, which has grown out of her experience and passion for caring for people. Lisa began her career in 1984 as a paralegal in a prominent Philadelphia estate planning and tax law firm. After relocating to California and working in a boutique pension administration firm, she began her own third party pension administration firm in 1988. She joined Washington Mutual Bank (WaMu) in 2006 and was there to support the Westchester community through one of the worst financial crises in our history. She remained with the WaMu staff as they transitioned to new ownership by Chase. After the merger, she went on to join JP Morgan Securities. As a result of this combined experience, Lisa brings a unique, compassionate, yet focused and practical approach to financial planning.

Lisa is passionate about empowering women through all stages of life. Women continue to struggle to find themselves and define themselves as worthy. As consciousness awakens across personal and professional lives, there is more and more chatter about having money and what to DO with it, and little to no conversation about the individual. The tide of marketing is still heavily about the money and what to do with the money; it has no connection to WHO is behind the money. A lot of progress has been made in creating financial plans by creating "deep" relationships with advisors. To Lisa, these are better than nothing, but in the end, they are only an inkling of what is really required to connect with one's inner value first. Women are absolutely artful and skillful at diversion, which has been required to survive and attempt to thrive in the evolving world toward equality. Lisa bravely stands beside women in such a way that women are free to explore their own inner landscape, define themselves to themselves, and create a plan that is not a "to do" but rather an extension of who they are.

Lisa is perceptive and sensitive to the transitioning that takes place between retirement and aging. She has the ability to smooth this bumpy road for her clients. She excels at beginning the conversations on the more difficult topics like dignity and death as facility diminishes. Her gift is her ability to instill grace and ease, while creating comfort with the uncomfortable. It is very common for clients to acknowledge her by thanking her for "saving my life." Over the years, she has come to see the deep desire of humanity is that of connection. As traditional churches and communities are in the process of redefining themselves, this space of disconnection and isolation is only exacerbated by outliving spouses, children, friends, and extended family. The prized legacy of leaving an inheritance for future generations is critically endangered by rising health-care costs and having strangers take them through the end-of-life experiences.

Lisa grew up on a farm in Pennsylvania. She brings with her an earthy and hardworking farm ethic to her practice. She attributes her ability to connect closely and deeply with individuals to this foundational upbringing. Lisa is deeply committed to the leadership conversation and supports individuals into being leaders of their lives and finances.

Lisa is currently writing two books and looks forward to publishing them in 2015. Her second book has the working title *Aging is a Team Sport* and seeks to empower individuals in preparing for the retirement and aging processes so that they may create the life of their dreams.

Lisa lives in Los Angeles and has two college-aged children, Kyle and Sara. They are her inspiration and balance. Because of them, she is heavily involved in education and mentoring. She is an active member of the Westchester Rotary and has served as youth services director where she has mentored and overseen programs for St. Bernard's High School Interact program, Westchester Enriched Sciences Magnet Interact program, and Loyola Marymount University Rotaract Program. She volunteers regularly to teach an empowering financial literacy program to schools and nonprofits, including places like Homeboy Industries. In her free time, she enjoys painting, writing, yoga, the arts, and other creative pursuits. She enjoys the California Central Coast and travels there routinely to renew and refresh herself.

From Lisa – What it means for me to be a Face of the New Feminine Leadership

To me, contributing to this book has been the raw reconciliation of my entire life. The intimate journey within has allowed me to step out and beyond my story. I have been gifted the opportunity to transmute myself and my story at an even deeper level. Out of the forge of this experience, I am emerging stronger and more alive.

It has been an honor to be included in taking and making a stand for Feminine Leaders. My desire is for the Feminine Leaders to be emboldened by embracing their fiery experiences, seeing their dross as burnt away and share themselves as the beautiful, gleaming golden inspiration they are. The conversation of feminine leadership born from victim to victor is a truly inspiring conversation. It is one that allows the sacred reframe of trials into the power of being Divinely inspired to make a difference.

The incredible process of witnessing other women plumb their own inner depths and claim their gold as they wrote and then shared their stories with me, has left me willing to be more humble, more vulnerable and deeply committed to giving voice to what has been longing to emerge for me and for other women in leadership for such a long time.

I look forward to celebrating with many women as they add their faces to ours. The countenance of Feminine Leadership is about to experience a face lift from the Soul out. I willingly bare my soul so that other women will have the courage and reap the reward of initiation and passage available in the pages of this book.

Connect with Lisa Margulies

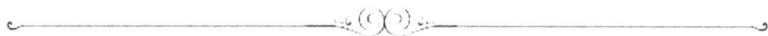

You can find out more about Lisa Margulies and connect with her directly here:

Email: lisa@regattainvest.com

Website: www.regattainvest.com

Facebook: https://www.facebook.com/lisa.margulies.79

LinkedIn: https://www.linkedin.com/pub/lisa-margulies/a/915/a84

Chapter Four

A New Pair of Shoes... For Each New Path

By Steffi Jo

Steffi Jo... An Amazing Feminine Leader

When I first met Steffi Jo, I was immediately moved by her depth and capacity to be present. It is a gift she shares generously, as she invites others to become more present within themselves. Knowing her as deeply as I do now, I am consistently inspired by her unshakable courage and commitment to keep growing as she helps other women do the same. Steffi Jo is a true feminine leader who exudes competence, confidence, and deep caring for the journey of a woman's awakening and expressing her essence. I'm excited for you to get to know this amazing woman! As she walks you through her journey, I encourage you to stay open and find yourself in her story as you walk your path in your own pair of shoes.

With love & inspiration,
Tracey

-4-

A New Pair of Shoes...
For Each New Path

***

I have come to a time in my life that what matters most to me are the answers to these questions: (1) Have I achieved what is most important to me in my life? (2) Have I given enough of my self to make a positive difference in the lives of the people I love? and (3) Have I left a legacy? There is strength and peace in knowing I have chosen only three questions to answer, but it has taken a lifetime of many questions and struggles to get here! I know the answers must lie in the same journey of the many paths I have taken with my heart leading the way. Within the simplicity of only three questions is complexity; the answers for all three questions are within the chaos of living and the outcome of the choices I make to bring order to a life's journey of walking many paths.

As I followed my heart, I had an understanding deep inside that the answers to all three questions are fueled by the same desire: my desire to understand how each of us are unique yet connected, and how we impact each other's lives in this world by the smallest of gestures and the fewest of words. I have also learned that my desire is not enough to find the answers. I must also look at the imprints of the steps behind me and the steps before me, and I must be willing to change my shoes to create new steps when a new direction is needed, always remembering that the feet inside my shoes are still mine.

As I look back at steps taken, I remember when I was a young girl of seven, and I had big questions. I am the oldest of four siblings; my mother was seventeen years old when I was born. We did not have a lot of money when I was growing up; in fact, for the most part, my three siblings and I shared one bedroom in a two-bedroom apartment most of the years I was at home. My father was in the military and came in and out of our lives. I learned how to take care of my siblings and myself at an early age. My mom held the family together and was the one who provided for us most of the time. My life started with a strong role model, my mom. I did not realize until recently how impactful the beginning of my life really was for a girl growing up to become a business owner and mother, among many other roles.

I learned in those early years that I had a desire to be independent. I would build forts under the heavy branches of the trees that lined the canal banks, and I would spend hours designing each room in "my house." I remember the feeling of being in control of my own space and having my "secret garden" where I could go and play and create a life that was mine where I would spend many hours each day.

I spent days creating adventures, not only in my "secret garden," but also indoors, when I would play with my Barbie Dolls for hours and days. I created very detailed adventures that carried on and on—another way to escape into a world without four small walls.

There was also another side of me that yearned to create something that others would want to buy from me. I made perfumes from anything I could find in the bathroom that had a sweet smell. I would mix the liquids together and fill up pretty little bottles that I collected to sell at my "perfume stand." I remember feeling accomplished and proud to put my concoctions out for others to smell and hopefully buy.

I realized how resourceful I was and how much I loved to make and create something from what little resources I had around me. I do not remember feeling deprived or poor; my mom had a way of making something appear new by cleaning it or remodeling it. I learned from her. If I wanted something different, I created it. I remember I would create my own world in which I lived separate from my siblings, perhaps because we were always so close, sleeping in one room, and I wanted my own space to breathe and call my own.

Looking back at the steps I took at such a young age, I realize now that I was more than greatly influenced by my mother. She set the stage for me to be able to pull strength from within. She taught me that I have everything I need within me. I just mold and shape what I already have to what I need; it is all there waiting for me. I did not realize how much this would shape my choices I made throughout the rest of my life.

Where does a young girl find her strength when she needs it most? For me, it was my experience of my mom. It was not so much what she consciously taught me; I really couldn't say she purposely taught me anything. However, she modeled it to me in everything she did. I learned from observing her. She was a young mother, yet she took on the roles of mother and father (most of the time) for me and my younger siblings. I saw her as a capable, strong mother working and creating a home for us. She never showed us that she might have felt overwhelmed or overcome by struggles of a young mother raising four children on her own. She just did it. I am so grateful for my learning because, without knowing it at the time, I needed to draw from her strength to survive the coming years as I grew into a teenager.

I had forgotten, for many years, that time in my life, and now I recall it with fond memories. It was a time that shaped my strength and my passion to help other women ignite their own inner knowing that they have everything inside them they need to fulfill their lives and their dreams. I can remember having a deep sense of something bigger than me, a vision of a purpose with no definition. I was still a young child, and it was just a feeling.

I remember looking down at my favorite shoes; I most vividly remember they were my white, shiny patent leather "Easter" shoes. They represented the steps of my young life that will remain imbedded with strength received from a young mother who ignited a purpose I would not realize until later in my adult life.

As I think about the pair of shoes I wore on my next path of my journey, it seems like a distant dream, one that I have laid to rest. However, it is a part of my life that brought me to this place of helping women to remember their strength, their dreams, and their voices. It was, without a doubt, fuel for my soul to follow my passions and desires.

This path was one of uncertainty and fear. My life changed forever, and I had bigger questions to ask. I searched for answers in very deep places within me. I asked myself, "Who am I? Why am I here? Why me?" and many more. It was an experience that seemed to pick me up and drop me into another world, one that has not been forgotten but has been forgiven.

I remember when my father was in our lives once again. His job took him in and out of our lives for all the years I remember growing up. I was still seven years old, my mother was at work that night, and I was awakened and molested. It was so unreal for me; it was as if I had left my body. It created a continuous string of conversations in my head that would continue for many years and into my adulthood.

I believe that the first path of my life, the one when I wore my white patent leather shoes, set me up to survive that night and others. I remember feeling, and knowing without words, that I would live through this experience. I had begun to take on the role of the oldest child, staying strong and helping to take care of my younger siblings; I then took on a silent role of protecting them. I was no longer the child I remembered. I was forced onto a different path until my early teen years. I remember walking in my child's shoes, but as I looked down, I saw shoes that I could not recognize or remember.

The conversations I had within my head kept some type of perspective that I held on to as I tried to make sense of it all. These conversations prevented me, when I was older, from falling into a victim's identity. I fought that helpless feeling with only the knowledge I had as a young girl. To this day I am not sure what I had inside that helped me to fight, other than the essence of who I am and those first years being influenced by my mother and her strength.

I went into a deep search for the meaning of life, of understanding the behaviors of people and developing sensitivity to my surroundings. I observed everyone, everything, and every place. I wanted to understand why people chose to do things. I wanted to understand why he chose to molest a young girl. I became very sensitive to feeling the energy of people and the energy of the environment around me. I had created an internal world of observation, and I began to develop a compassionate internal understanding of others, along with cultivating a very curious mind about people and their behaviors.

Over time I learned to forgive, and yet I had lost a part of me that had confidence and trust in the bigger world outside. I had built such a strong inner world of discovery, observation, understanding, and sensitivity of my senses that I could not always find the bridge from my inner strength to connect to my outer strength. That became the quest as I walked in my next pair of shoes.

I do understand now that without that experience I would not have opened up my passion of helping women to find their own strength and understanding of themselves from their past or to find what it takes to go deep within and to pull from the essence of who they are, in order to keep moving forward despite the challenges that are put in front of them. It gave me the tools to help others and to live my life on any path I choose with greater awareness and growth.

I left home at seventeen years old with my running shoes in hand. I had many adventures that took me around the world. On this path, I married my high school sweetheart, I gave birth to a very special and very stubborn baby boy, and I spent time in college as an artist. I also spent time living in my car as I drove and worked from coast to coast throughout the United States. I spent time in Pago Pago in the South Pacific, and I lived in Saudi Arabia for a few years. As I observed and lived among many cultures, my education and understanding of people grew immensely.

I believe that one of the reasons I developed my senses so keenly on my last path was my internal need to feel safe in my environment. I was able to find ways to feel safe and comfortable no matter where I ended up. During the time I traveled, it seemed as though my soul was taking a rest from the intensity of always asking so many questions, and I allowed myself to live more in the outside world—just live it. I experienced the world and different cultures, and I met people from all ends of the social spectrum. My love of observing and learning to understand others was brought to a new level by being outside the U.S. It prepared and taught me to listen very closely; otherwise, I would have missed the nuances of understanding the meaning behind the words spoken. This learning was priceless, although I did not truly appreciate what or how I was learning to listen until I began working with many people on a future path I was yet to experience.

Although it was a time of new adventures and getting in touch with understanding the world outside, I never truly left my internal life. I was resting from the questions I had as a young girl, but I had created new questions as a young mother facing the struggles I created, along with meeting a world bigger than the one I grew up in. I could feel inside me, at that time, I had a purpose and a calling greater than I could put my finger on. It created a space within me that kept me searching for my existence and kept pushing me forward.

By the end of this path, I felt I was rested enough and ready for the next ... my navy blue pumps!

I was still a young woman, twenty-nine years old, and I had already lived through many light and dark times and traveled the world. That little girl inside that loved to create and mix perfumes up to sell wanted to come out and play in a bigger world now. My husband and I created a new business, one that showcased his talent of understanding the general aircraft parts industry. We had no money, but we had an idea and an unwavering sense that it would work. We borrowed $5,000, and thirty years later, it is still a thriving business.

I used my talents for creating, marketing, accounting, administration, and being able to research and teach myself what I needed to know along the way. I read computer software manuals and taught myself how to create a database for our business. My mind was on fire and my heart was having fun! It was my love of creating something from nothing (or from limited resources) that fueled my learning to launch and operate our vision for this new company. I loved that time in my life because it fulfilled so many parts of me.

The learning over the next thirty years was priceless. I was challenged in so many ways: the fears, the ups and the downs, the successes and the failures, the emotional highs and the emotional lows, the laughter and the tears. Creating this business tapped into every part of my existence.

At that time, 1984, I was entering into an international industry with a niche that was new and innovative for the general aviation world. It was not embraced in the beginning by the "good ole' boys," but they were curious enough, and through the decades we have proven to be a model for many who have come and gone. It has been one of my greatest teachers of human behavior and inspired me to learn more about how to understand others and support them in their growth as well as my own. I had many opportunities to work with, manage, coach, and live through life experiences with many personality types through those years.

I brought my acute sense of observing and sensing the energy of others from my childhood into my work with the people who came and went from my company. It helped me to grow a desire and a passion to understand others, at even a deeper level. As the company began to get older, I was able to explore my other interests. I exchanged my navy blue company pumps and slipped on colorful wedges to skip into my next path.

It seemed for a while that I wore two pairs of shoes, my pumps and my wedges, as I lived a dual life. I operated and oversaw the company, and at the same time I was passionate about creating something from my heart and desires. The company was based on my husband's talents, and my soul was yearning to grow and express its own passions. As I raised this company and my children, my creative side was always a part of the mix. It seemed like I was always creating something: processes, procedures, new analytics or advertisements for the company, or something with my kids, after-school classes, family trips, parties, art and crafts. When time allowed, I would take classes and integrate new learning in areas of personal development for continued healing and growth for my family, my business, and myself.

As time went by, my energy and desires were directed toward creating a new business that would be based on my passions of personal growth, personal development, and helping others. My current company was running without me being there on a daily basis, my children were teenagers, and my creative self was looking and yearning to create again! It was a feeling of being called in a direction that I could not stop. I had not put words to it yet, but now I know that I was being called to fulfill my purpose. On some level it was a very familiar feeling that has come to the surface many times in my life, but I did not know what it was. Most of the time I would feel it as my creative calling, and I would paint or create something with the kids or do something new with my family, anything to satisfy the yearning within me. Yet the yearning would feel satisfied for just so long before it crept up again.

I felt my time had come, and I was ready to immerse myself in all my passions. My heart was full of expressions that wanted to come out. One of them was through my artwork. I connected my internal world to the outside when I created my art, yet it was not the whole picture. My art is created from a need to connect with myself that exposes my heart and helps me to connect to others. My bigger purpose is to connect with others and to help guide them on their own paths to healing from the inside out. My true purpose was only a feeling at this time; I had not yet fully understood what it was or how I would go about fulfilling it.

This is when another life event pushed me onto a path I did not see coming my way. I had to grab the strongest shoes I could find and as fast as I could ... so I grabbed my hiking boots.

Once again I needed to go deep inside and pull from the strength of that little girl and bring it forward to saturate everything I had learned through my life in order to make a decision that changed my family forever. This decision awoke a huge energy inside me that I now see as the true feminine strength that women have that can move mountains—if we allow ourselves to embrace that moment of that truth.

My husband was traveling a lot; he was in Europe at the time. I was taking care of the business, our home, and our teenagers. It seemed like it happened overnight; the signs were there, yet they were not recognizable until one day it hit me: I saw my youngest son caught up in drugs and he was drowning fast. My soul knew I had to do something fast or he would be gone.

Years earlier, when he was five years old, we went camping alongside a fast-running river. We were with another family, and we all went and stood with our feet in the water. My feet felt the sand as we enjoyed the cool water. My son stood beside me, and all of a sudden he was being swept away in the fast-moving current. I stopped breathing. In that instant time stood still. The water was muddy. I could not see him, but as I reached out, I felt his hand and grabbed it as he was floating past me and pulled him in, barely holding onto the river's bank. I almost lost my son that day; I was not going to lose him again, drowning in a world of drugs.

I pulled my strength up and made a decision to pull him away from his environment and his family in the middle of the night. Taking him by surprise, I sent him away to get help. He was fifteen years old. We did not see him until a year later. I held strong for him, my family, and myself. It was his journey, over the next eight years, to choose to recover from addiction or not. It was his family's journey of recovery and healing too as he came and went, in and out of our lives. He almost died in my arms more than a few times through those years. Today, he has chosen to live and thrive drug-free. I can only speak of walking my path through those years. My path was not his, but our paths were side by side through that time.

That experience taught me the power of my strength in a more intimate way than I had learned from all my other experiences in life. I learned that the true power of a mother's love must be to help give a child the strength to choose to live. I awoke to understanding I must lead as a model of compassionate strength that holds the knowledge and truth that we all have everything we need inside us to choose to live. I also experienced that being strong with compassion can also look like being a mirror for others to see the strength and compassion within themselves.

My passion to help others became even stronger through this experience, and I helped parents of troubled teenagers along the way. I realized that healing is personal and happens when we can go deep within, with no judgments of others and ourselves. It is a journey that we are not meant to do alone. Even if indirectly, our hearts can find healing in a gesture or a simple word from another, if we are open to receiving it.

It was time for me to move on to another path, and I purposefully chose to wear pretty little sandals. I was more open to the world around me and was ready to walk with myself more exposed. I opened up to another learning event, one of putting a stake in the ground. It was my time to create from my passions. This declaration led the way to another surprise path, one where I found myself alone. It seemed I still had something to learn before I could choose to lead with my passions.

It was a path of divorce. I changed into slippers as I took time to adjust and transition into a new life. Everything I had known and lived for more than thirty years was either gone or had changed: my marriage of thirty-two years, growing a business of thirty years, raising children, going through my son's challenge, and everything in between. I was tired and could have easily just decided to sit, rest, and do nothing. I had experienced so many paths; in a way I felt I was on a lost path now. I was tired. I no longer felt the strength I once had. I was feeling insecure about my life. My identity was all mixed up and fear was setting in. Feelings of, "I am not good enough, I am not strong enough, I am too old," swirled around in my mind. I was starting to spin out of control when I was stopped by the call of my passion and purpose once again. The familiar feeling in my heart once again came to surface and was holding on with strength.

This was another major event in my life, and I feel that by walking this one it gave me a perspective of life's transitions that I needed to understand, at a very deep level, to truly gather my strength back so that I may create my passion's vision.

I have followed many paths through my entire life and put on new shoes with every one of them. I learned many lessons and gained a lot of knowledge from all my experiences. This time, I must lead my path instead of following my path. I have gathered all my shoes in front of me as a reminder of the experiences, the learning and growth that I can call upon any time they are needed.

I held a different energy in my heart as I made the choice to lead my path and not follow my path. It brought a sense of continuity and wholeness to my life. I was able to see my journey made of different paths but all leading in the same direction and with purpose.

I choose to lead and model a life of a woman who has learned that life is not happening to you, it is happening for you. I have felt the strength of my life hold me in ways that I know came from the essence of my soul and was awakened by the strong women and experiences in my life. I speak of strength, not in the physical or mental capacity, but as a strength that only a woman can hold and give from her heart and her spirit. There is an awakening in this awareness, one of which I am passionate about helping other women see within their own paths and the journey they are walking.

My passion is also fueled by my love for my daughter; she is full of strength and beauty, inside and out. When I look upon her, I see a woman, a new woman of today's world full of strength and purpose, a woman who leads and inspires others. One of my greatest wishes is that I model for her what is possible when you lead your path from your heart. I feel a responsibility to carry my passion and purpose to the fullest extent for my grandchildren and generations to come. It is our daughters who will lead the world in change in the coming generations, and it must begin with women today having the courage to stand in strength, to be seen and to be heard, from the feminine essence within that has the power to move mountains. We need only make the choice to come out and lead other women to connect to their essence so that they may be role models for the women in their lives. One woman, one action, one word can lead change in the world.

Today, I am mentoring, coaching, and teaching women to connect to their own inner strength that has come from walking all the paths they have taken along their journey that has brought them to where they stand now. My vision is to help them see beauty in their essence and how they touch the lives of others by shining through from their hearts and their passions. We make a difference by showing up in this world, leading the way from the core of who we are and from the purpose we are meant to fulfill.

The goal that I will keep alive until I take my last breath is to always stay in process of answering my three questions:

- Have I achieved what is most important to me in my life? I will make choices in my life to live my experiences, understanding that each path has meaning and purpose for the journey I travel. When I finish my journey, I will have lived with no regrets.

- Have I given enough of myself to make a positive difference in the lives of the people I love? I choose to live my passions with conscious energy and positive actions, giving what is in my heart without holding back, modeling for my children and grandchildren a way to follow their own dreams by being true to themselves.

- Have I left a legacy? I choose to keep leading my path along my journey of being true to my purpose. My life has given me opportunities and lessons that I believe are meant to serve as a way to open my heart and my eyes to my purpose of helping others. I believe that we are not meant to be alone in this world. Each of us touches the lives of others in ways we are not aware of with each action and word we speak. I will choose to be conscious of my actions and my words because this is how we connect with others and model a new conversation that can lead to change in the world. I wish to leave a legacy that illustrates how one woman goes through life and chooses to learn from her experiences and to express her learning in a way that helps other women to do the same, as a way to strengthen the leadership of women—including young women and young girls—growing up to lead us in changing our world to be a better place to live in harmony.

- I was born a woman for a reason at this time in the world, when feminine leadership is being called to take a stand for change. My life has led me to go deep within myself with every pair of shoes I have worn and will wear, to find and live my purpose. On my journey, I found that we are intricately connected, and we have the power to change lives with one action or one word. We may choose how to use this power and how to react to it. I choose to make a difference by helping other women who are ready to understand the core of their essence and to embrace their place among feminine leaders leading the way of change in this world, one woman at a time ... one new pair of shoes at a time, for every path walked, until my journey is done.

About the Author, Steffi Jo

Steffi Jo was born in Oklahoma on Tinker's Air Force Base in 1955. When she was three years old, her family moved to Casper, Wyoming, for a few years and then, in 1960, on to Phoenix, Arizona, where she was raised and calls home.

She has a heart of a creator, an artist, and an entrepreneur. For over thirty years, she has co-owned a multimillion-dollar general aviation parts sales company. She helped to build this company from scratch to what it is today, a thriving company that has created relationships around the world.

She has had a very full, enriching life that has fueled her passions. Her love for her children and grandchildren has increased her urgency to lead her passion into action, and she founded Express Your Essence.

Steffi Jo works with women who are emerging, women who are putting the pieces together to create from their authentic essence and who wish to be congruent in all areas of their lives, inside and out. She works with women who have that knowing inside that their life is on a path of something greater than they are currently living, and they are coming out from behind what has held them back from reaching their next level of success.

From coaching to mentoring and teaching women how to truly see and understand their unique qualities and essence, she has an innate sense that helps women connect to their own knowledge of how they can create alignment in all areas. From dressing to branding themselves, to expressing themselves in any environment, she helps women create an authentic relationship with themselves that helps them to connect to and attract success, love, and abundance. She gives you tools to use that help you showcase the energy of your essence to support and strengthen your goals.

She also knows the value of renewing and replenishing the energy of her own essence. She loves the outdoors and has hiked over 350 miles in the Grand Canyon. She has hiked the ancient cities along the Italian coast and backpacked the American Samoa Island in the South Pacific. She has swam in the Red Sea and traveled through the Blue Mountains of Australia.

Steffi Jo is a multi-media artist. Her inspiration comes from people and how they connect to others. She molds into her paintings and onto the canvas with color and light pieces from generations past, as a way to connect the past to the present for future generations to see and connect to what once was.

Her gift is her passion to inspire women to connect with their own unique essence, to embrace who they truly are and express it from the inside out.

A Personal Message from Steffi Jo

https://youtu.be/kpcrr_3jRJE

https://essence2015.leadpages.co/free-gift9-steps/

From Steffi Jo – What it means for me to be a Face of the New Feminine Leadership

Being a "Face of the New Feminine Leadership" has brought a new meaning to my passion of helping and inspiring others. It brings a very clear message within me that I can truly honor and celebrate; it brings out the strength of who I am as a Feminine Leader. I am a model that I wish to be for my children, my grandchildren and beyond. There is no greater gift than being a model and a mirror of Feminine Leadership in today's world for other women to see themselves and the strength they have to be a change for themselves, their families and the world.

Connect with Steffi Jo

You can find out more about Steffi Jo and connect with her directly here:

Email: NewFaces@ExpressYourEssence.com

Website: www.ExpressYourEssence.com

Twitter: www.twitter.com/essencecoach

Facebook: www.facebook.com/ExpressYourEssence

Linked In: www.linkedin.com/steffijo

Chapter Five

Timeless Leadership, Millennial Style

By Alyssa Rizzo

Alyssa Rizzo... An Amazing Feminine Leader

Age means nothing except the ideas we place upon it. The true measure of 'age' is not really about time, rather it's about what one does with the time they have. The number is a symbol of life lived ... but not always. Alyssa has lived more life in fewer years than most people live in a lifetime. She is an extraordinary human being and old soul —wise, witty, and wildly acute in her ability to hone in on what is at the very heart of an issue, challenge, and solution. I'm honored to share this journey with Alyssa and to share this amazing woman with you. She is truly the face of the new feminine leadership, here to guide and lead multitudes across many generations into a deeper understanding of life, leadership, and living fully. Keep your eye on this lady. You'll love her story and know she's here for a mighty purpose...just like you.

With love & inspiration,
Tracey

-5-
Timeless Leadership, Millennial Style

I am young. I am bold. I have seen and experienced a lot in my life.

I have always been a scholar of leadership. When I was twelve, I started reading memoirs written by Holocaust survivors; I have always been fascinated by what makes people tick. When I was sixteen, I found a shelf that only had books on the topic of leadership at my local library. I devoured nearly every book on the shelf. In particular, I wanted to understand why certain individuals were more successful in overcoming challenges than others and even why some of them were able to then become impactful leaders. This hobby of studying leadership became my profession as I found a gap in my culture's understanding of leadership development. I felt that gap was holding our current leaders back from their full-fledged impact, effectiveness, and potential. I also felt that this same gap was stopping what otherwise would be qualified and capable individuals from stepping forward into leadership roles. As a result, I created a brand of leadership development that I felt was missing in conversations regarding leadership development.

I have three main points to share about the creation of my brand of leadership development: (1) how my own personal story became the foundation for my leadership philosophy, (2) the cultural and social barriers I saw keeping leaders from stepping forward in the United States, and (3) the method and mindset that I believe will help create effective and impactful leaders at every level from the neighborhood, to the boardroom, to global political offices to create powerful and lasting change.

Before I started living this purpose in earnest, my light was almost snuffed out. By age twenty-two, I was a three-time trauma survivor. I had a very normal, happy-looking, middle class suburban childhood: riding bikes with the neighborhood kids, learning to play piano, and dinner at home with Mom, Dad, and my brother. It was a great childhood with one exception: my mother was emotionally and energetically unstable. When she got scared, upset, or overwhelmed, her emotions would pour out in violent outbursts. Simple things such as not putting the dishes away correctly or not vacuuming when you were asked could result in a major meltdown; never mind the meltdowns when bigger things happened. As a result, I learned how to talk with someone in extreme emotional distress and calm them down. It was exhausting, but it was my way of surviving. No one outside our family knew, my father and brother had their own ways of coping, and I did not know any other type family experience: I considered it to be normal.

When I was seventeen, this parent made a threat to take her own life in front of me. It had happened numerous times before, but in the past I had never felt that it was a serious threat; it was simply a way for her to get the attention she needed in order to get her needs met. Over time, I became very good at distinguishing what was truly underneath any particular threat. I still have this skill. Despite my ability to understand what her need was beneath her threat, it was still terrifying every time she issued a threat, real or not. This time, her threat was real. I did what I had always done; calmed down her down and put her to bed. I was shaken to my core and this incident was the first of my three major traumas. At the time, I simply went on with my life; the scars were not addressed until later... much later.

I did not realize the impact this experience had on me until my second life-threatening experience. When I was twenty and at college, a very good friend made a threat to take her own life and the situation turned into a hostage crisis. Using the same skills I used with my mother, I was able to calm down the individual and neutralize the situation until the rescue team could arrive. Although everyone involved in this incident was ok in the end, I was brought to my knees.

My third trauma happened days before my twenty-second birthday. I was sexually assaulted by the person I was dating at the time. This trauma and recovery were much more nuanced than the others. Instead of being thrown into flashbacks and nightmares which had been my experience with the other two traumas, healing from this took a profound level of self-awareness, self-understanding, and self-forgiveness. This last trauma was the one that taught me how to forgive others and it was that skill that ultimately allowed me to fully heal from all my past traumas. It is the skill that still opens the path when I am stuck.

Trauma leaves deep psychological and spiritual scars. It robs you of you of who you thought you were and your sense of stability. The worst part is that it robs you of the hope that you can become a whole person again. This is true for psychological, physical, and emotional trauma. I had all three.

This story is not ultimately about trauma. It is not even about recovery and resiliency.

My trauma story and the self discovery that followed are the foundation of my philosophy of leadership development.

The journey of putting myself back together multiple times within a short few years offered me a level of introspection that many people have not experienced in their own lives. I attained a level of understanding of human behavior and a level of compassion that otherwise would have taken me many more years to develop. I learned to have compassion for myself as well as a deep level of compassion and understanding for those who harmed me.

Something very significant happens energetically, psychologically, and physically when your life has been threatened. After my second trauma, I was simply a shell of myself. Pre-trauma, I was an A student and varsity athlete with a razor sharp mind and wit. I was a leader in student government and other campus clubs. After my trauma, I was afraid all the time. I had trouble with my short-term memory. I could not stand to be alone in a room for any length of time. I became a nervous wreck every time I heard a cell phone vibrate. I lost my sense of humor. I had nightmares. I had flashbacks. The hardest part was that I never knew when they were coming.

The experience was like navigating a minefield every day. I never knew what was going to set my fear triggers off. When a fear trigger fired, I would have a meltdown. I woke up every day with a certain percentage of mental and emotional capital to meet the demands of the day. Some days I only had two hours of cognitive power, some days I had four. It was never consistent. Once that was burned out, I had nothing left. The only thing that would make it better was sleep. But sleep evaded me because it was filled with nightmares and cold sweats.

It was a very disruptive way to live, especially when I was in college. And I hated it.

Trauma changed so much of my identity, as it does for all of those who have faced it. Pre-trauma I was alive, vivacious, and energetic. The image of me as that young woman was gone. I literally could not remember what it felt like to be her. What scared me even more than losing her was that I did not believe I could ever get her back.

After a few months of this, I made a decision: I could not live like this. I was going to do whatever it took to get better. All the way better.

The gift of losing my cognitive functions was that I had to learn to trust my gut instincts. I had no choice but to develop this side of myself because the logical reasoning skills those of us high-achievers rely on did not exist for me anymore. I learned how to feel into my body when I was making a decision. I learned how to tune into it and listen if it was telling me to trust whether a decision was in my highest good or not.

The journey took a few years. As a result, I create a team of excellent trauma counselors, medication prescribers, and energy healers to help me as well as my family who had my back.

In order to reclaim my life, I had to face every single fear that I had. That meant literally going back through each memory, piece by piece, and neutralizing the energies, fears, and anxieties that were a part of my trauma experience. I had no other option. My fears were so disruptive to my daily life that I could not just ignore them. I could not turn around and blame someone else for my meltdowns. The only way to stop them was to comb through them, allow myself to feel what came up, and then allow my body to release the emotions and visions that inundated me.

As a result, I became an expert in neutralizing fear and working with intense emotions until they are released.

I understand when fear is so paralyzing that you can barely breathe. I have been there. I get it: Despite all of your best efforts and intentions, you literally cannot stop an outburst, a meltdown, or even a simple habit, like being late. I get it: Making a new choice feels like you are losing cornerstone pieces of who you are. I understand the bone tight fear that has you gripping onto something so tightly that you cannot let go even when it is crumbling down before your eyes.

Ultimately, what is the result of releasing fears? It is the first step on a journey of creating a new identity.

What I want to share with you is that when you release those fears, those old ways of being in the world, you have a remarkable ability to choose the kind of person you want to be. My trauma wiped out what it was like to be the old Alyssa Rizzo. When my trauma symptoms were gone, it was like I was handed a blank slate. I had the opportunity now to go on a journey of self-discovery. Who was Alyssa Rizzo? What was she all about?

I understand what it is like when you lose parts of yourself to a circumstance outside yourself. I also understand the process of letting go of old ways of being that no longer work anymore. My post-trauma self was not conducive for me to live a vibrant, happy life. I had to let go of her, in spite of the need I felt to still protect myself. I understand what it means to go on a journey of shifting pieces of self that were built so carefully for such a long time. I know how to manage the intense emotions and gripping fear and the pitfalls that happen during the journey rediscovery and self-rebuilding.

How does this relate to leadership?

This is the first piece that I want to leave you with: my own experience of losing parts of myself and having to claim a new way of being is the same journey that modern leaders face. There are two journeys that leaders must master to be successful. The first is walking through fear with grace. The second is the ability to shed old versions of oneself and one's identity in order to find deeper authentic pieces of self. Those new sides of self are crucial in finding new creative solutions to problems. The new sides of self that help the individual step forward with a new idea they never would have felt safe to stand behind before or of seeing a solution to a problem that was not available in their old mindset. I believe that the mastery of both of these processes the most important skill that is required for a modern leader to be effective, successful, and relevant.

You might not identify with my personal story, but there have been times in your life where you were unsure of the way forward as a leader. You did not know the direction your company needed to take. You did not know how to respond to a disruption from outside. I am sure there are times in your life where you have felt emotionally taxed and too exhausted to find a new way forward. I know that place quite well. I can lead you to the other side of it.

The first part of my leadership philosophy was created from my personal story. The second part was created from my travels all over the world. In college, I was blessed to be part of a study-abroad program called Semester at Sea. We traveled all over Africa and Asia. Some highlights included

Morocco, Ghana, South Africa, India, Vietnam, Cambodia, and China. Much of my time was spent observing the effects of poverty in each community I visited. In each location, I had the opportunity to connect with local community leaders who were working to help their community members, whether it was building businesses, education, or providing safe places for children.

One of my highlights was visiting with a group of musicians known as The Volcanoes in the South African township of Gugulethu, located just outside of Cape Town. The Volcanoes were a group of four or five men who played an instrument, sang, or danced. They generally played in local night clubs and were trying to make a living playing music. They explained to us how difficult it was to make a living doing anything—never mind music— in their community. These musicians were more than just players. They created a program for local youth to teach them music. In this community, music was a way to earn a living; it was not just a frivolous activity. The group had little to no resources by our Western standards. They had one keyboard, one drum, one speaker and microphone, and one trumpet. They worked with the kids in a cement building with only three sides. The third side and the roof were corrugated sheets of metal. Their choice to teach music with the resources they had redefined my understanding of what leadership really was. These men, who literally had nothing by my standards, decided to take what little they had and teach a group of local youth. This was the epitome of leadership in my mind. These men saw a community need: to educate children and give them a life skill. They compiled their problem solving skills and resources, including one piece of each equipment, and decided to share their time and teach local children how to be musicians and performers.

The special part of this story is that I saw it repeated over and over to varying degrees in each community I visited. I witnessed ordinary people who saw an opportunity in their community to do something that added to the overall health and vitality of the community.

All of a sudden, I realized that this was true leadership in action. These men did not wait for anyone to tell them what their community needed. They did not even hide behind the question of what resources would be required. They saw a need for the children in their community and they chose, very simply, to step forward and share their knowledge with those children. These men were not trained teachers. They had never put together a music education program before. They were not even formally trained musicians themselves. They did not look to others for direction; they simply took what they had, looked at what their community needed, and had an idea to fill that gap. One of the biggest lessons from these men was that they never felt that they needed to be someone they were not in order to serve their community. As a result, they became who their community needed them to be.

The second piece that I want to you to take with you is that the Volcanoes' example of leadership in their community shook me to my core. It was the exact opposite model of leadership than what I witnessed in the United States. Leadership has always been a cornerstone of American culture, starting with the Founding Fathers and their vision for America. Yet, despite our culture's focus on leadership, I saw a pervasive culture in the United States of capable individuals intentionally self-selecting out of leadership roles and responsibilities. Leadership was reserved only for "qualified" or "charismatic" individuals. The "qualified" are those who had built their own companies, created something due to their own ingenuity, or achieved great accolades for accomplishments in their field, such as Nobel Prize winners. Charismatic leaders are those who created great influence in large account due to the sheer force of their personalities such as Martin Luther King Jr. or President Kennedy. Who do you know who would dare to put themselves in the same category as such men? At the same time, I saw my culture vilify leaders who were stepping up in order to solve problems and create change. This is what I saw to be the current societal consciousness of leadership.

In the United States, we turned leadership into something that only a select few can really aspire to. The more as a culture we tried to understand the nuances of leadership, the more it drove away capable and talented individuals from choosing to be leaders.

Here in the United States, our institutions are in crisis, and leadership is the key to turning this around. This is no secret: from political gridlock in Washington to well-established businesses facing technology disruptions that render them obsolete within a few years. As a culture, we are facing more daily disruptions that do not always have obvious solutions while at the same time we still face many of the same challenges that have been with us throughout all of history. How many of us wait to step forward to address a problem in our companies or in our communities? How many of us hold back from stepping forward out of fear of criticism, or fear that we are not up to the task, or fear that our idea will not work?

As a culture, we are at a tipping point. How do we move forward when our leaders do not even know the path and there are less of us showing up for that job?

The first answer is that we cannot prepare for the unknown. But there are certain skill sets that make one more resilient, more adaptive in responding to crisis situations.

This is the conversation about leadership that I am having and I invite you to. The new discovery of self will support you in finding new creative solutions to problems. The new sides of self will help you step forward with a new idea you never would have felt safe to stand for before.

All of the work that I do with my clients is related to heightening their self-awareness. If you do not know where you currently are, how can you know where to go?

There is a fundamental difference between having created a leadership persona and having that leadership persona authentically represent who you are. Have you created a leadership persona based on who you needed to be in the past? Is that person you created still relevant to what is required of you now? Your leadership persona also must reflect your true gifts, not only the skills that you have learned to get where you are.

I have found that the greater the influence a leader has and the higher up in an organization they go, the MORE authentic they must become. This level of authenticity goes beyond simply "telling the truth." It encompasses the need to tell YOUR truth—as YOU feel it, as YOU see it, as YOU experience it. The only way to do that is to remove everything that is UNTRUTH out of you.

That is the journey that I take my leaders on. I help them shed all their layers of fear, of untruth, layers of who they thought they had to be in order to uncover who they really are. And then they learn how to be that person on purpose. This is what being a leader is all about. All the other skills more easily fall into place after this part of the journey occurs. The greatest part about this process is that it applies to leaders at every level: heads of companies, neighborhood leaders, and political leaders. It is the same journey, no matter where the individual sits.

The major piece that I want to leave you with is this: while our institutions are facing crisis after crisis, there is hope. As humans, we have remarkable abilities to problem solve, to think through an issue, to brainstorm with others, and find new ways forward. Yes, we are facing a time with more uncertainty than ever. That is why we need individuals who have the ability to access their internal talent on a deep level. Yes, there are basic skills to teach, but there is nothing that is more powerful than an individual who can dig deep into themselves to find a new way to look at a problem, to have the courage to bring them to light, and have the belief in themselves and their idea to test it. This individual must be willing to shed old ways of being to look at a problem in a new way. They must walk through fear to share their ideas with others and have the persistence to step back and reconfigure when their idea does not play out the way they wish the first time—or even the five times after the first time.

Key takeaways...

- Modern leadership mastery is not about accumulating more skills. As I continue to walk this path and lead others, I am certain that it is more about being able to connect deeply with your own self to find new ways forward.

- I believe we each have an "Inner Leader" and that's what propels us to become powerful leaders on the outside. The journey of finding your Inner Leader involves shedding layers of who you thought you in order to allow yourself to grow into something larger.

- Creating a leadership persona based on what you think a leader should look like, smell like, and feel like does not stay consistent with how an individual grows and learns. Uncovering your authentic self and then elevating that to a leadership level is the best way to be an effective and long-lasting impactful leader.

I am grateful to have turned the trauma in my life into the fundamental reason for my leadership philosophy and why I feel called to contribute to the global conversation of effective leadership. We have all experienced pain, trauma, fear and it is the transcendence of those places in our lives, as well as the tools to transcend those experiences, that allow us to be such a gift to the world.

I am grateful to have walked the journey myself to find my own Inner Leader. I firmly believe that all individuals called to leadership can walk this journey and it applies to leadership roles across the board including grocery store supervisors, corporate executives, youth sports coaches, heads of families, community activists, or even the President of the United States.

I believe you are here to make an impact, no matter what leadership role you have. I believe that you can find your Inner Leader. Join me in that journey.

About the Author, Alyssa Rizzo

Alyssa Rizzo is a leadership mentor and owns her own leadership consulting practice. She works with visionary individuals to become impactful and effective visionary leaders.

Her personal journey set in place her passion for effective, powerful leadership that comes from the inside out. Immersed in the study and experience of transforming trauma into healthy, compassionate leadership practices, Alyssa is masterful at honing in on the core issues holding back one's leadership potential.

Working with individuals, teams, and organizations, Alyssa is passionate about freeing the inner leader inside entrepreneurs, corporate executives, and community activists.

She strongly believes that each of us is here with a specific purpose, and transcending the trauma and baggage we all have is the key to discovering how we can best make our impact in the world.

Alyssa holds a BA in International relations from Simmons College. She plays a leadership role in a number of community organizations and is heavily involved in her church community. She has traveled extensively in Africa and Asia, specifically focusing on post-conflict work and poverty alleviation.

A Personal Message from Alyssa Rizzo

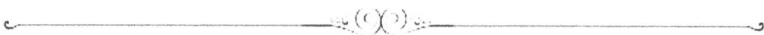

https://youtu.be/8MriIImvo2I

www.alyssarizzo.com

From Alyssa – What it means for me to be a Face of the New Feminine Leadership

Writing this book enabled me to fully acknowledge the importance of a new approach to being a great leader, as well as great leadership in general. As a fresh voice in this field, this book is my platform of introduction. By setting forth my knowledge and experience I now recognize the importance of sharing what I know with those who need it. It is through the fresh voices of those of us who have innate information about leadership that the world will be shifted for a great future.

Connect with Alyssa Rizzo

You can find out more about Alyssa Rizzo and connect with her directly here:

Email: info@alyssarizzo.com

Website: www.alyssarizzo.com

Twitter: https://twitter.com/rizzoleader

Facebook: facebook.com/rizzoleadership

LinkedIn: https://www.linkedin.com/pub/alyssa-a-rizzo/3b/507/28

Chapter Six

Self Love...The Ultimate Empowerment

By Leanne DiSanto

Leanne DiSanto... An Amazing Feminine Leader

There is a body that houses a heart. And there is a heart that is bigger than any "body" can be. That is who Leanne is to me. Her love for helping people and bringing out a new conversation that is more loving and kind about our bodies and ourselves is exactly what is needed now to change our world. She is a feminine leader who teaches what it means to love yourself and your body by leading with her own life first. I'm grateful to be able to share this amazing woman with you. She knows pain and possibility, and lives inside the conversation of transformation. I believe you will discover what's possible for you as you experience her story. I invite you to open and receive as Leanne shares her magnificent heart with passion, purpose, and pure love.

With love & inspiration,
Tracey

-6-
Self Love…The Ultimate Empowerment

———— ((•)) ————

I found myself on the closet floor with my husband's favorite sport jacket on. It still smelled like him—his cologne, his essence. A few days before, I got the call. … Craig had collapsed at a meeting, and the ambulance was transporting him to the local hospital. I arrived to a waiting room full of his colleagues and one unexpected guest, the hospital chaplain. I looked at him with a bit of confusion and said, "No offense, but what the hell are you doing here?" Feeling silly about my outburst, I giggled a little to hide my fear. He chuckled and replied, "They always call me for a heart event. The doctors are working on him now. We don't know anything yet."

Every tick of the wall clock's second hand sucked the oxygen from my lungs. Finally the doctor came in and cleared the room. "I'm sorry," he said. "He never regained consciousness."

"Please keep trying," I begged, but I knew—my husband of eight years was gone. As I lay curled up on that closet floor with so much sadness, so much disbelief, I thought, A widow at thirty-six. This can't be happening to me! And Craig, only forty-five! How? Why!

In the passing days I visited that closet often and felt comforted being near his clothes. As the memories flooded in of all our adventures—the big moments and quiet intimate times—my emotions felt like the flicker of an old black-and-white silent film. I moved from sadness to anger to joy to loneliness to disbelief all within seconds, holding thoughts for only moments before the next scene played. I cried, giggled, and said the "F" word a lot.

Then I was thrust into all the planning and preparations for his life celebrations. When I met Craig, he was a vice president for Burger King, then he continued on to run Coco's, Carrow's, and Denny's, restaurant chains. We had two memorials, one at corporate in South Carolina and one in California, and we had the funeral and burial in Connecticut, where he was from. It was a lot to handle, although I think that staying in action was a big part of the healing process for me. Receiving tons of letters and cards from the people that loved him, both professionally and personally, I began to focus less on my pain and more on the legacy he left behind.

Even with all that he had achieved, Craig was the humblest person I knew. When we would meet new people and they would ask what he did for a living, he would never give his title. He would just say, "I sell hamburgers." I would usually giggle and chime in with the real answer.

One of my favorite memories of his leadership and one that profoundly affected me is what I call the "Can I borrow a broom" story. Craig had just relocated to a new area for Burger King, and one day he decided to pay a couple stores a visit. As he pulled into the parking lot of this particular store, he felt the flush of anger bubble up at the mess he saw. Empty wrappers and cups littered the lot, which was a huge pet peeve for him. He felt that the first impression for the customer starts when they pull in and park. In the restaurant he witnessed similar disarray. Craig walked up to the counter and asked for the manager. A man came out from the back, and Craig said, "Hi, I'm Craig Bushey, your new vice president. Can I borrow a broom?"

The manager replied nervously, "You want to borrow a broom?"

"Yes, can you grab me one?" He continued, "When I'm outside sweeping the parking lot, can you clean these dirty tables and refund the money to the tables with customers, please." With broom in hand, leaving a very scared manager behind, Craig proceeded to clean up the parking lot. He never went back into the restaurant that day. He just knocked on the window when he was done, smiled, waved goodbye, and leaned the broom against the door. The incident was never mentioned again, and that restaurant became the best producer in the region.

The way he handled that experience, as well as others over the years, had such an impact on me. He taught me that we can't always control what is happening or the situation we are in; we can only control our reaction to it. Sometimes the best reaction is no reaction … just showing up with an open hand and open heart and saying, "How can I help?" I got that true leadership is service.

My life as I knew it was over, and I had to forge a new path. Like my memory of the "Can I borrow a broom" story, I couldn't change what happened—only my reaction to it. I trusted that there was just a different path for me now, and that God doesn't give you anything you can't handle. So in that place of trust, I felt my grief turn to gratitude. With each passing day and month and year, when sadness creeps in, I shift it to a deeper sense of thankfulness. Craig would often say to me, "I can't believe you picked me." So now I say, "Thank you for picking me. It was an extraordinary ride!"

"Life is not measured by the number of breaths we take, but by the moments that take our breath away."
-Anonymous

As a personal trainer for over twenty years, I've worked with thousands of clients all over the country. Craig and I had just moved from California to Atlanta three months before he passed. I decided to sell the house we had bought and move back to California. In the nine years we were together, we moved from Atlanta to Chicago to Dallas to London to Greenville, South Carolina, to Newport Beach, California, and back to Atlanta, where we had met. I'm from Massachusetts originally, but California felt most like home.

We were only back in Atlanta for a couple months before Craig passed away. Within a few months after that I resold the house we bought and with the love and support of amazing friends, I was back in California.

Craig and I had actually decided that we would end up back in California, and after he was done in the corporate world, we would buy a couple restaurants for him to run and a gym for me.

I continued on that path, and Fitness Patrol, Private Training Studio was born. I knew I wanted to do it different from and better than the big clubs that seem more interested in selling memberships than in true transformation. With multiple degrees and certifications, I was armed with the knowledge, but it was my personal experiences with extreme dieting and training for bodybuilding competitions that brought my heart, empathy, and understanding. I was excited to create a space where people could come not only to get a kick-ass workout but also to feel safe, understood, and part of a community. I knew that more went into this journey than just "calories in calories out" and how many push-ups you can do. I knew it wasn't about just putting clients on a diet and exercise program and all their dreams would come true. We are in a relationship with our bodies and with food, one that changes and evolves as we do.

My journey as a bodybuilder and national fitness competitor had taught me that going to such extremes does not only mess with your metabolism but with your mind and self-worth. Extreme dieting set me up to yo-yo in my weight and yo-yo in my mind. Once in the restrictive, deprivation mindset, nothing but perfect is good enough. That perfection showed up as, "Well, I already had one cookie. I might as well have the whole box and be perfect tomorrow." So there I was again, after another binge session, feeling like, "What the HELL, Leanne!! You know what to do. Why aren't you doing it?"

I was keeping it together on the outside, but inside I felt like a fraud when I wasn't walking my talk. Even in that, I wasn't granting myself grace. I could have compassion for everyone else but not always for myself, not for that little girl that lived inside me that just wanted to be loved, perfect or not.

I grew up getting a lot of attention for my looks—some wanted attention and some unwanted—although when I was younger, I'm not sure a really knew the difference. At thirteen I looked eighteen, and I joke that I had boobs before you could buy them. So I guess it is no surprise I choose to compete in a sport that is all about how you look.

"You can't change the wrapper without affecting its contents"
-Dr. Phil

During my bodybuilding days, I used competing and getting ready for a show as my motivation to get back in shape, so I knew that just focusing on a short-term goal was not the answer to a sustained level of health, energy, and vitality. I knew that short-lived results from being too restrictive just leads to disappointment and shame.

At Fitness Patrol, I offered a more integrated approach, one that was more about lifestyle and long-term results. To say you're going "on" a diet implies you will be going "off "a diet at some point. So I didn't prescribe diets. My programs were based on healthy eating and integrated, functional movements. My team of trainers and I worked with a variety of clients ranging from age twelve to seventy. Some clients wanted to lose weight and tone up; some were competitive athletes; others wanted less stress and a greater sense of well-being and energy. Even though our clients were getting great results, with some, I was seeing guilt, shame, and disappointment in their efforts.

Every Monday would roll around, and it was like sinners to the confessional. ... "I was so bad this weekend." ... "I didn't work out." ... "I couldn't stick to the plan." I called them "Confession Mondays." Although I heard things like these on a daily basis, Mondays were the worst. I would do my best to reassure and motivate, but I saw the self-judgment and criticism. I could see that the best eating and exercise plan couldn't erase the underlying beliefs or inner critic, and even when my clients hit their goals and transformed their bodies, there was no pot of gold at the end of the rainbow. The happiness you would expect was not always there.

I started to feel that I had it all wrong, that there is a flaw in the whole fitness industry—not only from my own experience but also from what I was seeing my clients go through. With a master's in exercise physiology and multiple certifications, I've been trained to know how the body works, how the body moves, and the optimal way to fuel the body, but there is a critical component left out. I began to see that it was really about 20 percent mechanics and 80 percent psychology. Our thoughts, feelings, and beliefs are the drivers for all behaviors and the choices we make. These beliefs run so deep at the subconscious level that we don't even know they are in play. I started to see that some clients may never feel that what they accomplished was good enough unless we considered the whole person.

I felt like I was suffocating under these negative conversations: "Yes I lost weight, but I still hate my thighs." ... "I had some fries last night—I'm so bad." ... "If I could just lose five more pounds, I'd be happy."

I get that I was a trainer and my job was to help people transform their bodies, but I was seeing more and more that it was counterproductive and counterintuitive to address just the body without looking at the whole mind-body-soul connection.

I was growing and changing and seeking deeper answers for myself and for my clients. I started to feel disconnected from what I was teaching. Although the strategies were sound, I was resonating more with the fact that you don't have to count calories to live a life that counts!

At my core, I want to help people to honor and to love who they are. I wanted to have a new conversation—a different conversation, one that is less about what you eat and more about who you are as an eater and one that leaves the what I "should do" and what I "shouldn't do" guilt behind. All the experts are shouting at each other, but very few are stopping to look at the bigger picture.

I began studying people such as Tony Robbins, Wayne Dyer, Marc David, Joe Dispenza, Marianne Williamson. I looked at how our thoughts create our reality, and I was finding so much passion there that I decided to sell Fitness Patrol and step away from personal training. As I was evolving, I felt the pull to speak and lead in a different way and to serve at a higher level.

During my years at Fitness Patrol, I remarried and had my beautiful daughter, Francesca. Unfortunately, the marriage did not work, and I was going through a divorce during this time of transition in my career. So again, I was in a whirlwind of change and again felt that God must have a different plan for me. Although that relationship did not work, I believe we were brought together to have Francesca. For that, I will always be grateful, and my ex and I remain good friends today.

> *"Faith is taking the First Step even when you don't see the whole staircase."*
> *- Martin Luther King Jr.*

I found that the more committed I was to stepping out as a leader and expert, the more resistance came up in subtle ways. I didn't even recognize it as resistance. It showed up as confusion, self-doubt, procrastination, and perfection paralysis. I was wishy-washy in my commitments to myself. I was not living consistently everything I wanted to teach. I was great at keeping my word to other people, but not always at keeping my word to myself. Nothing erodes confidence like not keeping your word to yourself.

I couldn't let any fears or doubts stand in my way. I was seeing these old patterns for what they were—a way to keep me safe, a way to keep me from being vulnerable.

On one hand, it was perfect that all these feelings were coming up for me because it was in line with my message. Everything starts with awareness; then you can make a choice based on what you say you are committed to.

I was committed to getting on stage and speaking my message, and I was aware I needed support. That is when I met my coach and mentor Tracey. Through her programs, coaching, and unwavering support to hold me at my highest, I realized I had everything I needed and that I am my message.

Every good coach has a coach. I would always say that Michael Jordan was the best at what he did, and he had coaches. We are all in this human experience together and need support. I have always been a leader; I'm just leading in a different way now. My own growth and evolution will never stop. I am a lifelong learner, and with every client that I get to serve and help transform, I'm transforming right alongside them.

Transformation is like dusting … it's never done. Transformation is a living, breathing thing in our lives. Unlike a goal that is set and achieved, transformation is a deeper knowing. Sometimes it's a big, on-your-knees moment, when you say, "Not one more day am I going to do this or think like this or live like this." It can also show up as a whisper or a nagging sense that "I am meant for more than where I am right now. I will not be defined by my past or by what the scale says or by what is in my bank account. I am more than my current circumstances, and I have the power to transform whatever is not working in my life by being responsible for my choices and standing in my truth."

Transformation is a moment-by-moment choice. It is not only a moving forward but a reconciliation and a releasing of the old way of thinking and being, a letting go of beliefs and actions that don't serve you at your highest.

Imagine you're looking into a kaleidoscope. Right before the beautiful image comes into focus—it's hard to make out—but beyond the blur you can tell that there is something magnificent. There have been times in my life that I lingered in that blurry space a little too long, and other times, with a quick millimeter turn, I was able to see the beauty, grace, and infinite possibilities.

What blurry spaces are you living in? What one decision, choice, or commitment could be your millimeter? Are your reactions to the world around you based in love or based in fear? Are they based in consuming or in contribution? The smallest, subtlest change or adjustment can make all the difference today! We are never as far away as we think; one empowered choice leads to the next, then the next.

"When would NOW, be a good time"
-Tony Robbins

My work and life are now dedicated to helping you feel empowered in your body, to leave a life of deprivation and lead a life of inspired choice. Being empowered in your body is about aligning how you think, eat, and move with your deepest desires and life intention. When you are empowered in your body, you are empowered in your life.

My passion is to show you a new way of experiencing your life, to bring more joy and freedom to the choices we make every day, to create a body and life filled with energy and vitality and a deeper sense of love and connection to ourselves and to those around us. I go deeper so that you can SHOW UP in all areas of your life and become aligned with your true self.

I start exactly where you are now ... no more regrets, no more guilt, no more beating yourself up. We just START.

Key takeaways...

Thoughts~Feelings~Actions~Results

Thoughts live in the head, feelings live in the body, and often they are not linear. It's like what came first, the chicken or the egg? It's been thought (no pun intended) that thoughts happen first and then a feeling is generated, although I believe it is more circular: they influence each other all the time. Based on these thoughts, we take action and produce a certain result. So if you are not getting the result you want in some area in your life, look at your thoughts and your underlying beliefs. Beliefs are just thoughts left unexamined. We can have up to thirty thoughts a second. Who says they are all true?! It starts with asking better questions: Instead of saying, "Why does this always happen to me?" ask, "What can I learn from this pattern of behavior, and what can I do differently?"

Vision + Structures + Support = Change

Any change that you want to make in your life starts with awareness, with declaring what needs to change. You need to have a vision of what you truly want, you need to put structures in place, such as daily rituals that are in line with your vision, and you need support from a coach or a friend that keeps you on track and accountable. Identifying these three things—vision, structures, support—is vital for sustainable change to happen, whether it be changes to your body and health, your relationships, or your career and money.

Goals vs. Transformation

For me, goals are more about WHAT do I need to "DO" to achieve something? Transformation is more about WHOM do I need to "BE" to live the life of my dreams? What do I mean by this? Take the goal of wanting to lose weight. You set the goal and figure out that you need to eat a certain way and exercise more. You put a plan in place for what you need to do to achieve that goal, but it's more about what is outside yourself. When you look at it as really wanting to transform your body and ask yourself, "Who do I need to be to make these changes?" you are seeking the answers from within. It's being responsible for your choices and in integrity with your word to others and to yourself. It's a higher intention and vibration that goes beyond food choices and exercise programs.

Everything in life is a lesson

I have learned that no matter what has happened or is happening to me is a lesson. It's all part of my life apprenticeship. Like Maya Angelou says, "When we know better, we do better." We can't always control what has happened; we can only control our reaction to it. What sends you into the deepest despair or triggers you the most is your greatest teacher. Recognizing those moments for what they are with no judgment and being able to shift will bring you the greatest sense of peace and freedom.

About the Author, Leanne DiSanto

Leanne has been a certified master trainer and fitness expert for over twenty-five years with a master's in exercise physiology. As the founder of Fitness Patrol Personal Training Studio, she has helped thousands of clients transform their bodies and their lives through education, motivation, and inspiration.

Leanne's own personal journey with deprivation dieting and extreme training as a former bodybuilder and national fitness competitor led her to understand that traditional strategies alone will not bring sustainable results. This prompted her to go deeper in her own life so that she could better serve those around her.

Now as a certified life coach, Leanne bridges the gap from where you are, both physically and emotionally, to where you want to go. You no longer have to feel shame and guilt around your body and everyday choices. Her Empowered Body, Empowered Life philosophy teaches you a comprehensive approach by aligning how you think, eat, and move with your health and fitness goals and your life vision.

Leanne brings her extensive expertise, as well as her special mix of life's lessons, compassion, and humor, whether she is working one on one or speaking to a large audience. Her passion as a coach, confidant, and cheerleader is sustainable transformation and an unwavering dedication to stand for you in your greatness.

She gets it and she gets YOU!

A Personal Message from Leanne DiSanto

https://youtu.be/XvP9VEdnfo4

http://leannedisanto.com/book

From Leanne – What it means for me to be a Face of the New Feminine Leadership

As a feminine leader my hope is to be a lighthouse for women to come home to themselves...and for them to know that they are their own lighthouse of awareness, awakening and attraction. To embrace all of your past as your sacred journey and know it doesn't define you. All of the blessings, lessons, struggles and tragedies have been the seeds that have helped us grow and blossom into who we are today. For me, in this process, I have cultivated and strengthened my roots truth, faith and self-love and have worked on releasing and letting go of the weak roots of self-doubt and fear. My hope for "Faces of the NEW Feminine Leadership" is that every woman who reads it can open up to who they really are, know they are not alone and shine like the lighthouse they are!

Connect with Leanne DiSanto

You can find out more about Leanne DiSanto and connect with her directly here:

Email: leanne@leannedisanto.com

Website: www.leannedisanto.com

Twitter: twitter.com/LeanneDiSanto

Facebook: www.facebook.com/Leanne-DiSanto-913693148694428/?ref=tn_tnmn

LinkedIn: www.linkedin.com/pub/leanne-disanto/31/66/914

Chapter Seven

Loving our Kids: Inside of Us and Out in the World

By Sharyn Henry

Sharyn Henry... An Amazing Feminine Leader.

A woman can only be as believable as her commitment to herself. She has to be the example in her own life to have a meaningful impact on others. Sharyn is such a woman. She is truly amazing! Her work with kids, horses and parents is groundbreaking and essential to creating the next generation of leaders who will bring our world to a better place. This woman not only walks her talk, but she trots her truth in such a magnificent way that only a real feminine leader can. I'm grateful to share this brilliant lady and I know you will "gallop" along with this amazing woman who is real in her story and fierce in her commitment to teaching our kids to love themselves and lead the next path.

With love & inspiration,

Tracey

Loving Our Kids: Inside of Us and Out in the World

It was never spoken. It was never held over me. I was never forced to conform. I actually never even thought about it. But I grew up thinking that I had to be a certain way to be loved.

We never discussed how we felt. We just did stuff. We were a busy family of four, active in the usual sports, school, and youth organizations. My parents were always the leaders and successful in all they did. They made changes as city leaders and board members, they were high ranking in corporate America, they volunteered for youth organizations, and they set an example of serving and success.

There was tension in our home; I'm not sure why. I do know that I became the peacemaker in my family, mediating between my parents, my brother, and myself. I felt the need to excel to fulfill unspoken expectations. This undercurrent kept me busy, and I became wonderful at orchestrating success for the family, myself and how I presented myself to the world. How the world saw us was more important than who we really were.

What was on the outside became my reality, not what I felt inside. My inner turmoil, which I didn't even know I had, eventually showed up, bubbling out of me in the form of sickness. It turns out my family's physical weakness shows up "in the gut." This was the case for my parents, my brother, my cousin, and now me as I was diagnosed with ulcerative colitis, a very unpleasant, painful, and incredibly inconvenient disease that ulcerated my large intestine. It ruled much of my life. It totally sucked to be different. My reality now was as the sick kid—another new identity I didn't ask for. How I felt physically became my reality; it ruled.

It was hard growing up being sick all the time. I was different and it wasn't fair. I didn't talk about it with my friends because it was embarrassing. I felt ashamed. On the outside I looked completely normal. Inside I hurt, physically and emotionally. It was hard being a teenager and I didn't fit in anywhere. I wanted so much to feel worthy. I wanted to be loved and cherished for the real me, the one I kept hidden. I wanted to be accepted.

I've always had a love for animals and a passion for horses. They are so regal and so gorgeous. They have such raw power wrapped up in busy ears, a flowing mane, and a soft muzzle. Horses were a huge part of my life growing up. We had many in our backyard, and I loved taking care of them. I learned everything about horses that I possibly could— how to care for them, ride them, and compete. I was an avid equestrian, a horse lover, and I found peace in their presence. They gave me a place to belong and that became my identity.

I fit in at the barn—no judgments, no acting, total acceptance. I could be myself. As I grew older, I was still lost. I was looking for me in activities, other people, my career, through two marriages, and through my kids. I needed them to affirm my value because deep inside me was this hole I needed to fill. I never felt like I was "enough." If I could be externally beautiful, keep everyone happy, be the peacemaker, be good at everything I did, then I had value. I was accepted and "loved" because of my talents. I was truly superwoman—I was all that and a bag o' chips!

I became so good at pleasing other people, filling my time, and being who I thought I was that I looked for who I was through others' eyes. My identity was based on other people's perceptions of me. Myself, me, moi... we were a jumbled mess.

Who was I?

The one thing that has consistently served me throughout my life is my willingness and openness to improve, grow, and develop myself. Because of the ulcerative colitis, I learned to pay attention to how things affected me. What I ate, my stress level, how I handled various situations, they all played a part in how I felt physically. As I learned how my body reacted, I began to see a connection between controlling my thoughts and how I felt. This awareness opened me up to seek myself bit by bit, year by year, more by more.

My identity has always been tied to my love for horses. Throughout my life, the horses have always been a place for me to feel grounded, a place to be myself, to be raw and open. The completeness I felt when I was with the horses as I was growing up and developing as a person gave me the anchor that I needed. Time stood still when I was at the barn, whether I was riding, cleaning corrals, organizing the area, or just being still.

Because of my training over the years with the horses and the gifts their presence gave to me it was natural for me to want to share my knowledge and my experience. I volunteered for many years at a local youth organization with kids that owned their own horses. We connected easily because of our shared passion for horses and my ability to relate to them on their level. I truly enjoy kids; their openness, curiosity, innocence, willingness, and dedication are such a treat! The most significant treasure I received from giving so much to these kids was the gift of nurturing the little girl inside me that could so easily relate to them and where they were in life.

Looking back on my own childhood, I know the healing the horses offered me and the empowerment I felt because of them. I was the queen of my castle, or at least the head cowgirl of my barn! This was an area I could learn to master, a place where I could feel a sense of control in an out-of-control world. Knowing this, feeling this yummy space, loving and relating to kids... it took one friend to point out my gift, and my road to teaching about horses and paralleling it to life was paved.

This was my life's purpose.

One of my pitfalls that was a theme throughout my life, even with my passion for horses, was that I was still looking for others to validate who I was as well as confirm my value. My need for love and acceptance from other people was all I knew. It wasn't until I realized that I was doing the same thing over and over, repeating the long-time patterns and expecting a different outcome, when I had that moment of... "This shit isn't working anymore," that I realized how tired I was. Tired of feeling empty. Tired of feeling alone when I was with someone. Tired of relying on others to affirm me. It was too much work! I asked myself why I would put so much effort into a friendship or a relationship just so that they could affirm my value when I could cut them out of the middle and put the effort into me? I decided to discover me, date myself, and learn to be alone. I set out on a journey to heal, accept, and love myself.

It was my time.

My courage to step into this unknown came from deep inside me. A little voice was whispering, "What about me? How about you care for me? Will you please take care of me?" And I finally listened. I was fed up. It was time for change! It was time to take care of myself, to learn about the parts of me that felt so empty, to be still, to be quiet, and to heal. It was so very natural as a daughter, as a wife (and later as a girlfriend), as a mom, as an employee, as a _____ (you fill in the blank) to put myself, my care, and my needs aside. But I knew there was more planned for me, that I had a greater calling, that the world needed me in a bigger way.

I knew in my bones that I was destined for more than where my current path was taking me. With this in mind, I signed up for a conference designed to teach me how to do speaking engagements about the gifts my horse riding and teaching business give to kids. I already felt comfortable speaking in front of people when it came to the content of my presentation, but knowing how to get in front of the right audience and where this would lead me was a mystery. I just knew that I needed to be there. That decision changed my life.

I learned several things at Tracey Trottenberg's conference. We all come from messed-up lives to varying degrees, but what we do with it is what matters. I was shocked as each person shared about their life and some of the horrifying experiences they had lived through. I was further surprised at the successes they created in spite of their challenging histories. I felt a deep admiration and knew that I too could create a life that I dreamed of. Tracey created a safe place for me to open up, took me deep with gentle questions, and showed me that everything I needed was inside me. All I needed was the guidance, the support, and the courage. The fears I carried weren't so different from the fears everyone else carried.

She modeled a new way of healing that took me to my core and gave me the tools to heal. This was a new beginning for me. It was an awareness that opened me up and planted a seed. One that continues to flourish day by day, choice by choice.

Six months after my speaking conference, a new opportunity with Tracey crossed my computer screen. I knew something was missing, and I knew I needed the support to make a change. When this opportunity presented itself, I knew I had to be there.

It was at this conference that I drew a line in the sand. It was scary. It was an internal struggle. Say yes to me? What?! But I knew that this was what I needed to do. My gut instinct said to dive in, so I shoved the doubts and fears aside and took the leap.

I was open, I was vulnerable, I did the work, and I put in to practice over and over the things I was learning. Through this process I invested in myself for the first time, and so began my evolution. Over the next few months, I learned to trust myself, heal old wounds, and take care of the little girl inside me. I feel like I've blossomed into the woman I was meant to be, and my journey is a gift I can use to help others.

I've found when people work with horses something inside them shifts. Many feelings arise: fear, awe, tenderness, peace, excitement, curiosity, intrigue, joy. I would dare to say everyone with a pulse has some sort of reaction when they see a horse run with the wind whipping through its mane, when they witness the tenderness of a mother and her foal, see the kindness in their eyes, touch the softness of their muzzle, and feel their warm breath. Their size can be daunting at first, but over time that can be replaced with a feeling of accomplishment, of being empowered by learning the skills to work alongside the horse as its partner. Horses can teach us so much about ourselves if we know what to look for, tune into our feelings, and consider what they mean.

They are grounding, healing, and accepting, and connections can be formed with them that don't always happen in a human-to-human relationship. Through my riding programs I help parents raise a new type of youth, kids that are learning that life is much bigger than themselves. Around the horses they are required to be aware and follow certain rules to stay safe. They are introduced to a new type of communication.

They learn to read a horse's body language, the uniqueness of each horse, and they learn to adapt. The variance of how the student has to "speak" to the horse on the horse's terms—these are skills for life! These communication skills are easily related to communicating with their peers, parents, and others in the world.

Horses also need to know that their rider or handler is someone they can trust. A horse will look for their human to "lead" them and keep them safe. The horse also needs to know that their rider is in charge, or the horse may take advantage of their rider. The student is forced into a position of learning to be the authority or leader in the relationship. It's incredibly empowering for a young person to master each step of their time around the horses. Working with them on the ground, saddling, and riding is the beginning. Then they master control of their horse in a variety of situations and through the walk, trot, and canter. Some kids go on to compete and enjoy the challenges and successes that it brings. It's a unique dynamic that empowers a one hundred-pound person to control a one thousand-pound animal, and it's oh, so fulfilling.

All kids need to have every opportunity possible to learn about themselves, to feel empowered and confident, to have the inner strength to be our future leaders. Working around the barn, mastering horsemanship, learning the nuances of communication with others, being responsible for themselves, and having an awareness of how their actions affect others are some of the ways the students grow from the inside out. And they're having fun in the process! There's nothing like a game of tag on horseback to test all these skills!

The passion I have for coaching kids using horses is so obvious to the kids and their parents. They want my help. They share and recommend me because of the transformations they witness in their own child as well as others' kids. The joy and love shared among the students and myself is palpable. I give them permission to be themselves and meet them where they are. We connect on a different level, and with the trust that's built between us, I can teach them the life skills they need to be empowered.

Parents and I are working together to grow a new type of youth. Our world needs kids that are leaders. They need to be respectful and filled with inner strength. They need to know how to communicate, have a strong work ethic, be resourceful and be aware. The programs I've developed for our youth utilizing horses are growing from the grass roots of my barn and touching lives worldwide. I model a whole new type of teaching for kids of all ages.

All kids need to know they are perfect as they are. They don't have to be smarter, funnier, skinnier, fatter, or more muscular. They don't need to have a different hair color or a different skin tone. They don't need to be rich, poor, or somewhere in the middle. They are each unique and lovable—as is... end of story! Their inner dialogue should be filled with "I can," "I am amazing," "I am so lovable," and "I matter." Their view of themselves should be full of respect and filled with self-love, so much so that they model it for others with their love, kindness, patience, and groundedness.

It's so delicious to envision schools filled with self-assured young ladies and gents: a new generation of youth that is mindful, kind, hardworking and aware; youth that can understand the ripple effect of what they do, how they speak, and their beliefs. We need a new generation of kids that have the tools to communicate, be confident in their abilities, and also be aware of their weaknesses. This self-awareness could open their minds and help release the fears that can stop them in their tracks.

My horses and I are changing lives. It's so exciting! We're teaching and supporting parents in raising their kids and making a positive impact on society, one person at a time, bit by bit, stride by stride. The kids that grow up with my mentoring at Red Hat Cowgirl are moving on in life as examples of well-rounded young adults excelling on the paths they choose. Our children look to us to love and guide them. Parents look to us to educate and empower their kids. Society needs our help.

Deep within my soul I can see the far-reaching effects of the model I've created. There's a drive within me, a heartfelt mission to share what I've learned and witnessed with my students and with other horse trainers so that they too may ride along on this path. My mission is that through the teaching that I've created, all children around the world will have the opportunity to learn about themselves, be empowered, and burst with self-confidence through working with horses. Kids that are solid on the inside are our future. They are the leaders.

Key takeaways...

- My differences and struggles taught me what I otherwise wouldn't have learned.

- Everything I ever needed was inside of me. I just needed to make the decision and get encouragement and the tools to take the leap.

- Dating myself was a gift and a journey.

- All our children, especially the children inside us, need to be loved, healed, and recognized.

About the Author, Sharyn Henry

Sharyn Henry is the Red Hat Cowgirl, a horseback riding teacher specializing in using horses to empower her students. As far back as she can remember, she's been a horse-crazed kid, but now she's that same kid in a much older body!

She's been an avid horsewoman for more than forty years, riding several different disciplines, and studying with 4H, Pony Club, and various riding coaches.

Sharyn remembers well the life skills she learned growing up riding and the self-confidence it fostered. Horses gave her a purpose beyond school that was a wonderful place to belong. She knows firsthand the powerful connection we have with horses and what they can teach us about ourselves.

As a mother of three and an active participant in their activities, Sharyn saw the benefits of their work around the horses. It was a natural transition to share the same opportunities with their friends.

From that point forward, her purpose was realized. Her expertise and personal experience with horses and kids grew into combining the two to teach life skills. Her teaching has continued to touch more than 250 kids over the years.

Sharyn helps kids from all walks of life learn about themselves, become strong communicators, become confident, and grow from the inside out. And that's straight from the horse's mouth!

A Personal Message from Sharyn Henry

https://youtu.be/iuu11ImZp14

www.redhatcowgirl.com/book

From Sharyn – What it means for me to be a Face of the New Feminine Leadership

This book was an opportunity for me to reflect on my journey and relive it. It was a celebration of how far I've come! My belief in myself, the gifts I share and the impact I have truly are a blessing. It's my hope that women reading my story will see themselves and it will give them encouragement and hope to rewrite the path they're on. It can be easy to base our value on all of the external portions of our lives, yet the reality is that everything we need is inside us. Love, happiness and courage is my gift to you.

Connect with Sharyn Henry

You can find out more about Sharyn Henry and connect with her directly here:

Email: redhatcowgirl@yahoo.com

Website: www.redhatcowgirl.com

Facebook: www.facebook.com/redhatcowgirl

LinkedIn: www.linkedin.com/in/sharynhenry

Chapter Eight

Smiling From the Inside

By Allison Watts

Allison Watts ... An Amazing Feminine Leader

A love affair of purpose and heart, Allison and I connected deeply on every level from the first moment we met. Her commitment to transform the health industry by teaching each dentist, doctor, and practitioner to value the precious individual sitting in their chair is so very needed right now. Willing to do whatever it takes to become the feminine leader that she is today, her passion for growing into the highest expression of what's possible in human compassion and care inspires me deeply. Her steadfast spirit is just the beginning of what makes Allison an amazing woman. I believe you'll agree as you experience her journey and feel the possibility of the change you too can make in your own life, family and work in the world.

With love & inspiration,
Tracey

Smiling from the Inside

It's as if I'm not even here. I'm sitting in the orthodontist's office as he projects giant pictures of my face, teeth, and jaws from every angle and explains to my parents all my facial defects and all the reasons I need braces and jaw surgery so that I can be and look "normal". I'm eleven years old. Sitting in his office, I feel frozen, numb, and in shock. When I get home, I can't stop crying as I look in the mirror and see myself as ugly for the first time. On top of feeling ugly, I feel exposed, like everyone else can see this defect and they know something is wrong with me. I've known something is wrong with me, but I've been able to hide it—the insecurity and anxiety, the feelings of not being wanted, not being accepted, and not being okay—those can all be hidden, but this can't. Now everyone knows there is something wrong with me.

Only a year before this experience with the orthodontist, I found out I was adopted. And now this. No one knows how broken I feel. I just want to feel safe, loved, accepted, and normal. I want so badly to feel okay about myself, but now there's a new layer of fear and insecurity on top of what is already there. And I'm only eleven.

I think my defects make me unlovable, so as I go through school and life, I figure out ways to get people to like me and accept me. I make a decision to excel at everything I do, to be smart and funny so that people will accept me and like me and maybe I'll even accept me and like me. I find ways to compensate for my "defects." Becoming an overachiever and making sure I am a leader in everything I do seems like a good strategy, so I adopt it. Underneath the façade is my overwhelming need to prove that I'm okay, to show people—including myself—that there is nothing wrong with me. I try to distract myself from the painful feelings inside by doing things to make me feel better and by pointing out other people's flaws, hoping they won't notice mine. It seems to be working, and I'm pretty sure I look like I have it all together.

As I finish high school, it's obvious that the best career path for me is in the health professions. As I complete my college degree in pre-med, I look at a few specialties in medicine, but after going through life-changing braces and jaw surgery, I know dentistry is for me. I want to transform lives the way mine was transformed! I want to help people feel more confident and love themselves by giving them a smile they feel good about, like braces and jaw surgery did for me. Fortunately, I have the grades, the drive and the qualities and characteristics that make a good dentist, so I go to dental school. Even though dental school is challenging, I like it because it is another way for me to prove myself to the world, and it moves me toward my dream of changing lives.

The summer before dental school, I marry the man of my dreams. He supports me in every way as I go through dental school. My third year in dental school we have our first child, a precious baby boy. When I get out of dental school, I choose to start my own practice from scratch and my husband fully supports me through that, too. My first year in practice, we have a precious baby girl. These beautiful children are definitely gifts from God and I do the best I can to be a good mother and wife and to take care of everyone, including myself, but the practice seems to pull so much of my attention. I travel a lot to attend continuing education classes because it will get my practice "there" faster and then I will have more time for everything else. There are certain things I will not sacrifice because I know how important they are, so I make sure I attend all of my children's school functions, sporting events, and after-school activities. Even though I show up physically, often I'm not there mentally and emotionally. I'm sure my family can feel my lack of presence, but I don't know what to do about it. When I'm not working in or on the practice, I'm thinking about where it needs to be or worrying about staff, money, patients, etc. I am really struggling to integrate all the pieces of my life, so it feels like my work life is very separate from the rest of my life, and work is eating up more and more of my time and energy.

I am so driven to excel and prove myself competent as I go through school and now as I build my practice that it has become a pattern. I am obsessed with proving myself and feeling successful in my work and as a result, I am much more tuned into my masculine characteristics than my feminine nature. My values of personal power, freedom, and excellence are overriding my values of health, family, and spirituality. For many years the feminine side that wants love and connection and wants deep relationships with others and myself gets ignored. I am not connected to myself, my heart or the things my heart wants. During this time, I am not taking good care of myself physically or emotionally, and I don't take the time to stop and smell the roses or examine what I'm doing and why. I also don't take the time to recharge and reconnect because I don't realize I need to--this pattern is costing me a lot, but I can't see it.

Very early in my practice, I hire consultants and create an inspiring vision, and with my team on board, we are well on our way to creating a comprehensive esthetic and restorative practice that changes lives. I am definitely on the fast track to realizing my dream practice! It is very exciting, but as I chase this dream and push through all the challenges, I feel like I'm forced to put all the other parts of my life on the back burner. I just keep telling myself it's worth it and "When I get my practice established, I'll have the time, energy, money, etc. to devote to my family, God, my health, and the other areas of my life."

At this point, I am miles away from my true self. I don't even know who my true self is. I am trying to create the self I want to be by being like people who appear to be successful and happy. I believe if I can be like them, I will experience the confidence and fulfillment they seem to have. As I become more disconnected from myself, I become more disconnected from everything and everyone else. This is not working out well for me and it is definitely not getting me what I really want, but I believe it will, so I keep on going. The pain and emptiness inside are growing but I ignore it and push through like I always do.

When my team and I reach our vision and we finally have the practice we've been working toward for over ten years, it feels great. We worked hard to get here, and we have truly created a wonderful practice. I have dentists telling me they wish they had a practice like mine and asking me how I did it. I enjoy this accomplishment for a short time, but the joy quickly fades as I realize how unfulfilled I actually feel. I begin to question my noble mission and all the sacrifices I made. I feel alone, lost, and guilty. After all, I should be happy because I finally have the practice my team and I worked so hard and sacrificed so much for... the practice I always wanted, a practice any dentist would love to have. From the outside it looks like I have it all together, but inside I am struggling. I feel depressed as I realize the price I have paid for "success" and I know I can't continue like this.

Now, after over ten years in practice, I'm feeling like my mission failed. Or did it? I reached my goals—a level of clinical competence and the "successful" practice I had aspired to. I realized my vision and mission for my practice. But I am not experiencing what I thought I would experience when I got what I wanted. I don't feel the way I thought I would feel when I "arrived." What does "arrived" mean, anyway? I begin to question my beliefs, the value of having a vision, what a vision really is, and where it comes from. I begin to question my choice to focus so singularly on my practice at the expense of everything else and to keep driving toward that vision without stopping to celebrate successes, enjoy the journey, and make sure I am heading in the direction I really want to head.

At this point, I haven't created a new vision in years, so all of the sudden I don't have one. The chase ends, and I am lost and directionless for the first time. This is a scary and strange place to be; it is very foreign to me and my team after so many years of having such fierce purpose and drive. My husband wants to help me, but he doesn't know how. I don't know how to ask for help, and I don't think he understands anyway because it's "practice related." I feel disconnected again.

As I grieve the loss of my dream, I begin to see that most of the things I've done to try to feel fulfilled, the courses I have taken and the practice I have built can't give me what I've been looking for all along; they can't fill the void inside me that I have been trying to fill. Much of the work I've done up to this point has been focused solely on practice success, not my life. I've been looking at "successful" dentists and what they are doing to achieve success and trying to emulate that. I've been focusing outside myself to figure out what I need to do to feel successful and spending little time and effort working on the inside; my thoughts and beliefs. I do believe the things we do on the outside are important, but clearly mastering those does not equal true success and fulfillment.

I begin to think about what really does lead to fulfillment and success. To me, true success is having a rich, fulfilling spiritual life, exceptional health and wellbeing, and having true connection in our relationships. I have always wanted those things, yet my drive to build a successful business has dominated my life. Below the surface, there has always been a relentless, unconscious drive to feel competent and confident, a need to be good at what I do because I think my value comes from what I do. I'm also driven by my values, my personality and my need to heal people's wounds, especially those affecting their self-esteem. I am beginning to see that I will need to find ways to become aware of and overcome these unconscious needs and drives because I know that if I keep doing what I'm doing, I'll keep getting what I'm getting and I don't want that. At this point, I'm seeing that getting help and great role models is important for me--role models for how to have the marriage and relationships I envision, role models for how to be the mother I dreamed of being, and role models for how to be truly healthy and spiritually connected--all while running a successful business.

In light of my new awarenesses, I decide to change directions. I get new coaches and begin taking different kinds of workshops and courses. As a result, I have three big realizations: (1) My business is not where I get my worth; I have innate worth (2) deep, lasting change and fulfillment come from the inside, and (3) I can and must find a way to integrate and balance the different areas of my life. A new vision begins to emerge... one where I am in my practice in a healthier way and I am integrating all the pieces of my life. One where I am moving toward something instead of running away from my "broken" self and trying to prove I am okay. One where I see people as okay just as they are instead of projecting my own need to be fixed and healed on them.

I went into dentistry because I wanted to change people's lives and I am able to do that by giving them exceptional health, beauty, and function. I also want them to experience a sense of confidence and self-love as a result. It doesn't always happen, but I do get to change a lot of lives and it is very rewarding. I have had many experiences of changing people's lives on many levels and realize that we never really know which levels we are affecting. Sometimes giving someone a beautiful smile can transform their entire life, and sometimes it's just one layer. It depends on the human being that is sitting in our chair and the experiences they've had—sometimes it has little to do with teeth. In any conversation in any setting, the person in front of us has layers of things going on, and we get to decide how we show up, how we see them and how deep we are willing to go with them. I can't control how others respond, but I can control how I show up in the relationship and in the conversation, so that's what I choose to do. In my practice, it's a given that we provide excellent dentistry, but even more importantly my team and I choose to show up with compassion and a willingness to listen and understand what our clients really want and why they want it. In my practice and in my life, I show up with the intention of connecting with people at a deep level, and I support people in creating deeper, more lasting change from the inside.

Every single one of us has the power to impact how people see themselves and how they see their situation. We may be consciously aware of that power, we may be completely unaware of it, or we may be somewhere in between. We use our power when we speak and act, but much of it comes from how we see ourselves, how we see the other person, and what we reflect back to them. I realize now that the way I come to each person I'm with—the way I see them and regard them—is deeply important. When I look at someone, do I see what's wrong, or do I see what's right? Do I see people as broken and defective, as someone who needs to be fixed, or do I see them as perfect just as they are with the choice to be, do, or have more? Is my role to fix them or to guide them to be their best selves and reflect their greatness back to them? How we see others affects how they see themselves. Many of us are taught to be experts at seeing what's wrong. Many of us believe that our clients come to us to tell them what's wrong and to give them solutions. Many of us believe that at least part of our role as parents is to help our children understand what they are doing wrong so they can avoid mistakes and be the best they can be. And so many of us see what's wrong with our spouse or partner much more than we see what's right. Is that empowering? Is that what we want our role to be? Is that really what is asked of us? Or are we called to something higher?

I believe we are called to and we can choose something higher--to see our clients and everyone in our lives as human beings, "perfect" just as they are. I believe that we are actually here to help people see their greatness and challenge them to be the best they can be. Imagine people coming for our services and leaving feeling great about themselves in every way; imagine every client leaving feeling better than they did when they walked into our office. One of my patients told me that when we went through the comprehensive exam process with her to create a vision and plan for her long-term oral health, it led her to think about her vision for her whole life and the kind of mother and wife she wanted to be. She said this process changed her whole life, and we hadn't even done any dental work yet! There are more stories like this, and there is no limit to the impact we can and do have on people. In our personal lives, we can help those around us know and experience their own greatness because of how we regard them. Can you see how this applies to all relationships, inside and outside of work?

Once I realized that no matter what we do, our success in life depends on how we relate to other people in some way, I could see the importance of interpersonal skills. Connecting with people on this deeper level, with who they really are, may take practice and work for some of us. In fact, despite "evidence" that women are naturally in touch with and good at emotions and feelings, I wasn't. I have really worked on my emotional intelligence and interpersonal skills because it didn't come naturally to me. I was very out of touch with my emotions and how to be with them. I was also uncomfortable with the emotions of others. Once I could see the value in developing these abilities, I chose to work on this. I am living proof that we do not have to be naturally great at communication and relationships; it is a skill that can be developed!

To develop these skills, to be truly present with others, and to help them feel safe and work well with them, we need to do our inner work. Doing our inner work helps us connect more deeply through what we say and do as well as who we are being. The better I get at being present, listening deeply, and working on all aspects of leadership and communication, the better my practice and life get. The more I learn about and connect with myself, the better I connect with everything and everyone else. The more I connect with everything, the better life gets. It all starts with me and how I choose to show up and with you and how you choose to show up.

Can you see how we can transform all our relationships just by how we perceive things and how we show up? If we are intentional about this, we can create more fulfilling, empowering experiences for everyone we encounter (including ourselves). I believe this is what life is really all about. Because of the inner work I've done over the last ten years and the exponential results it's created, I've grown to love leadership, personal growth, and communication even more than I love dentistry. Even though I believe it's very important to deliver excellent dentistry (or whatever it is you deliver), I don't think it matters as much as our ability to connect with the unique human being whose life we have the privilege of impacting. If we don't understand them and where they are--their circumstances, personality, values, hopes, and expectations--many of them won't allow us to do the great work we know how to do for them. And for others, even if we do get to do the work, it may fall flat or they may end up unhappy or not following through because we didn't get to the root of what they really wanted and expected and why they wanted it. For me, if I don't connect with the human being I'm working with, my work feels empty.

Whether it's natural for us our not, my invitation is for each one of us to be aware of the power we have to impact people and choose to be intentional about using it for the good of all. As I sat in that orthodontist's office so many years ago, he did not realize the impact he had on me with his words, his actions and with the way he "saw" me. He certainly didn't know how insecure and fragile I was. None of us know what's going on for the person in front of us and what's below the surface, but we can assume everyone's got wounds and challenges and pain—it's part of the human condition. Because of this, there's a reverence that is appropriate in any conversation and in all relationships. It's a way of being with people wherever they are, whatever they say, and whatever they are feeling. We don't need to be counselors or therapists, but we do need to realize that people come with things that affect our ability to relate with them and we can either learn how to work with those things or pretend like they don't exist.

To work with them doesn't mean we have to do anything; we just need to be aware of and be responsible for what we're saying and doing and how we're being. We need to make it safe and hold the space for them and whatever is going on for them. It takes practice and awareness, but it is so worth it! As doctors, we took the Hippocratic Oath to "First, do no harm." This is a big responsibility and it doesn't just mean physically. We can unconsciously do harm emotionally if we're not aware of our power to heal or to hurt people. This is one of the biggest reasons we would choose to work on ourselves, so that we can be aware of and learn the skills to be with people no matter what is going on for them. Learning to be with our own emotions is the key to being with the emotions of others. If we can't be with people's fears, anxieties, and needs, they can sense that and are likely to feel misunderstood, unsafe or judged by us even though that's not our intention.

As I have come to see the value of working from the inside out, my mission has evolved from changing people's lives to helping people transform their lives from the inside out. I believe this is the only way to lasting transformation.

Mastering my thoughts and beliefs (what's going on on the inside) and helping others do the same, as well as creating structures and systems for success (on the outside) has now become my passion! For years now, I have spent most of my time and resources learning these skills and helping others learn these skills. In fact, several years ago I chose to become a certified life coach so that I could help people create true and lasting success—in their businesses and their lives. After twenty years in practice, I am now transitioning out of my dental practice and moving into full-time coaching. My dental practice has provided me the perfect place to do what I was meant to do for the last twenty years and to learn all of these wonderful lessons, skills, and tools so that I can now help others have the impact and results they are meant to have.

Now I help my coaching clients connect with themselves, their clients and everyone in their life at a deeper level. As my clients do their inner work, they find greater clarity, experience deeper and clearer communication, and they find they are more present and more intentional in all areas of their life. Since business is only considered successful in the context of a happy life, we start with the vision, beliefs, skills and structures for a great life. Then we begin to work on the business. I love helping health-care providers create a practice and life they love from the inside out. It doesn't just impact the people they work with and the patients they serve, but it affects everyone they come in contact with and the impact goes out exponentially from there.

Our results come from our behavior and our behavior comes from our thoughts and beliefs. That's what makes the inner work so powerful. If we work on our beliefs and what's going on on the inside, it affects everything we are experiencing on the outside. We've all heard, "Know thyself". This advice from many wise sages is considered long-established wisdom because the wisest people know that our perception and beliefs affect our results and our experience of the world more than anything else. If we want to create different results, the biggest bang for our buck is working on our beliefs. Understanding and knowing ourselves is powerful and is a journey of a lifetime, so I continue to work on it. I invite you to do the same because it serves everyone when we are being our best selves, and being our best self gives others permission to be their best selves.

As I am continuing to move forward on this path of self-awareness and self-mastery, I now have an opportunity to be truly congruent on an even deeper level. In the past, much of my effort was focused outward as I built my practice and then strove to give others the love, acceptance, and understanding I thought they wanted and needed. What I didn't realize was that I was actually giving them what I most wanted and needed, the gift of love and approval. It seemed to be serving everyone, but things were way out of balance because I was ignoring my own needs along the way. Then I realized it wasn't selfish or wrong to ask myself, "What about me? When and how am I finally going to get the love and acceptance I need? Who's going to give it to me? Who's going to fill my cup?" and everything changed.

It became crystal clear to me that I'm the only one that can truly fill my cup. It's my responsibility and it's my time to make sure my needs are met and that I allow myself to receive those things. What a freeing and empowering realization! This has transformed every area of my life, especially my relationships. By loving me, I'm giving others permission to love themselves. I'm showing up differently in all areas of my life—more powerfully and more connected. I'm more tuned in to me and to others than I've ever been.

Not only is it not selfish to take great care of myself, but it is imperative because if I give myself the love and approval I need, then I'm no longer looking for it "out there," and that neediness cannot rob me of the opportunity to be truly present in relationships and conversations. Also, if my needs are met, I can be fully present and available to listen and really "be" with other people. I can also give a lot more when my cup is full. More and more, I'm listening for and to my own voice, quieting all the other noise and allowing myself to have needs and wants without judgment. It's very different because I've been listening to other people and looking for things outside myself to make me better and more successful my entire life. I've ignored my true feelings and my true self because I thought others knew better than me what I needed. Listening to outside voices and what the world was telling me I should do and be didn't work for me.

I can also see another thing that has kept me from feeling happy and fulfilled was the lens I have been looking through. The beliefs, "There is something wrong with me" and "I need to be fixed and healed," had me always seeing what was wrong with me and constantly searching for ways to fix myself. They did not allow me to experience feeling whole, okay and loved. They were affecting how I showed up in every area of my life. I knew that if I continued to do that, I would never be happy and fulfilled. In fact, it was taking me farther away from my true self. Now it's time to come home; it's time to listen to me and create the life I was born to live.

When I got these lessons, everything shifted. I believe I never would've gotten them if I hadn't chosen to work with coaches. My coaches have helped me become aware of things I never would have been aware of without them and that has led to my exponential growth. I've been working with coaches for over ten years now and it helps me be at the top of my game so that I can help others be at the top of their game.

These are some of the things I've learned and some of what my journey has taught me. I share this with you in hopes that it will serve you and make your journey easier; that you can see yourself in this and be inspired to do whatever you need to do to trust yourself, to hear your own voice clearly and loudly, to identify your own wants and needs, to ask for them knowing that you deserve to have them met, and to realize that you are the only one who has the power make it happen. Then I hope that you will help others do the same. The more we learn to do this and help others do it, the easier it gets. Change starts with me and you. I'll continue to work on myself, and I ask you to please do your work, whatever it takes! And get whatever support you need. You are here for a reason, and the world is waiting for you to fulfill your mission; it is waiting for all of us to step up and be who we were meant to be! At my core, I believe I was meant to have the experiences I've had exactly as I had them; that the terrible experience at the orthodontist so long ago as well as all my other experiences, good and bad, have made me who I am today and have led me here so that I can make the difference I'm here to make. It feels like I am finally stepping into what I was born to do.

My vision is that everyone on the planet knows what a powerful creator they are and that they know that they can choose the life they want to live and create it.

My vision is that every woman feels connected with God, herself, her mission, her partner, her children, and her life. My vision is also that—one doctor and one patient at a time—we transform lives and health care to be a more empowering and inspiring experience for everyone involved. We should heed Jesus' famous words when he says, "Physician, heal thyself." It starts with me, and it starts with you. No matter what field we're in, it starts with us working on and healing ourselves because that's how we can show up as our best selves and help others do the same. The way each one of us shows up and the way each of us leads our life and our business matters. This is the beginning of a new era and a new conversation in dentistry, health care, and on the planet! We are ready for a new way of being where we are responsible for how we show up, for what we say and do, for who we are being, and for the impact we have on people.

Together we can create a powerful wave of change, a new way of thinking and being that will impact not just health care, but every facet of our lives. Will you join me?

My takeaways:

1. Knowing what's below the surface, what's driving you, is important for your success.

Do you know what drives you? Do you know what are you chasing? Or what you are running away from? Are you looking outside yourself for something? Will you find what you are looking for there?

2. We have a lot of power to impact people (including ourselves) with what we think, say, do, and feel. It's about how we show up and who we're being.

Are you aware of the power you have? Are you using it intentionally? Do you know the impact you are having on people and how you are making them feel? Are you aware of how your own beliefs, thoughts, words and actions are making you feel and the impact you're having on your own life? Are you consciously choosing?

3. For long-term success, listen to yourself, your needs, and your wants without judgment, and give yourself unconditional love and approval (or whatever you've been looking for) and allow yourself to receive it.

Do you know yourself? Do you know what you need and want to be truly happy? Are you creating ways to give it to yourself? Are you able to receive it?

About the Author, Allison Watts

Dr. Allison Watts is a restorative and esthetic dentist who has maintained a private, fee-for-service practice in Midland, Texas, since 1995.

Allison has always enjoyed continuing education at the highest level and has completed the majority of the continuums at the Spear Institute, the Dawson Center, and the Pankey Institute. She has been a member of the visiting faculty at the Spear Institute and is visiting faculty at the Pankey Institute. She has served on the advisory board at the Pankey institute and is a member of the alumni association at Pankey Institute and the Dawson Academy. She is a member of the ADA, TDA, Permian Basin District Dental Society, and the AGD. She has participated in study clubs for years and is currently in a Spear study club and a Pankey study club and has served as an advisor and been a member in her local Seattle study club for years.

Allison is a speaker and a certified professional coach with the Ford Institute and the John Maxwell Team. She enjoys coaching dentists (and other health-care providers) to be their best selves and to bring out the best in their team and patients. She enjoys mentoring dentists as they implement the principles and skills they learn at the Pankey Institute, the Dawson Center, and the Spear Institute. Allison is involved in a progressive program at Baylor College of Dentistry that offers dental students and alumni leading-edge information on comprehensive, relationship-based dentistry. She also enjoys working with dentists to increase case acceptance so that they get to do more of their best and finest work. As well as working with dentists individually, Allison also enjoys presenting and leading workshops in the study club setting. She is the host of a monthly teleseminar titled, "Practicing with the Masters," where she interviews leaders in the fields of dentistry, leadership, and practice management to bring some of the best information available to dentists, their teams, and other health care providers to help them create a practice and life they love.

Allison has been married to her husband Daniel for twenty-five years and has two beautiful children—Coleman, age twenty-one, and Lexi, age nineteen. She loves her family, including River, their chocolate lab. She enjoys activities with her family, reading, personal development, all types of exercise, dancing, nature, and health and wellness. Allison loves helping people change their lives and create a life they dream of!

A Personal Message from Allison Watts

https://youtu.be/km-oQCcDV-4

http://transformationalpractices.com/book/

From Allison – What it means for me to be a Face of the New Feminine Leadership

Being an author is an honor and it is an even greater honor to be a co-author with this group of amazing, powerful women! I have known for a long time that I had a message inside me and that I would write at least one book. For me, it's part of my calling; it's a way for me to do what I am here to do: help people see how powerful they truly are and help them create a life they love and be who they were born to be!!!

Connect with Allison Watts

———⋅ (( )) ⋅———

You can find out more about Allison Watts and connect with her directly here:

Email: insight@transformationalpractices.com

Website: www.transformationalpractices.com; www.allisonwattsdds.com

Twitter: www.twitter.com/loveurpractice

Facebook: https://www.facebook.com/Transforma-tionalPractices;
               https://www.facebook.com/allison.watts2

Linked In: https://www.linkedin.com/pub/allison-watts/8/60a/4a

Pinterest: https://www.pinterest.com/awattsdds/

Chapter Nine

Where We Go From Here and Why Your Voice Matters

By Tracey Trottenberg

Where We Go from Here and Why Your Voice Matters

Just like the women in this book, your time is now.

Your voice matters, and everything is a stage. We don't believe that you flip on a switch to become a speaker or leader by title. Rather, it's who you're being all the time, wherever you go, with whomever you encounter. It's in your presence and in the experience of what it's like being around you, not just what you say or espouse. It's about your capacity to connect and be present and authentic in your communication and conversations. Not perfect, never perfect. But in process. This is what attracts all the people, wealth, opportunities and stages to you. It is what creates real impact.

This takes learning to trust yourself, speak your truth and share your story. It requires a willingness to be seen and expose yourself and your deepest heart for a greater purpose than what keeps you small and hidden.

This takes real courage and commitment, because it is scary and tempting to 'get off the path' every time it gets bumpy.

And, it takes a community of like-minded people to support and hold you accountable to your greatest expression and greatest self.

All of this creates freedom and pure joy! And, if you're anything like me and the women in this book, it's what your soul yearns for. It's what is often called the "choiceless choice": you know deep within that you're meant for more, and you have a desire to share a message that must get out there.

We want your voice and story out in the world too! You are needed, now. It does not matter who else is speaking a message or leading a business similar to yours. The fact is there are people who will only hear the message from you. They are praying for you to share your wisdom and humanity, your brilliance and bruises.

The New Feminine Leadership isn't just about the fact that biologically, you're a woman. Sometimes a man embodies these feminine qualities more than a woman. We've seen this in business, politics, entertainment and media. As we mean it, this is about being a woman who is willing to lead from her heart and use her head to support what she knows 'below the neck'. A woman who digs in to reveal and stay true to her innate nature of love, kindness, power, joy, passion, and wisdom. She's smart, savvy, strategic, and spiritual. She's a woman willing to be seen in her glory and her guts.

She's a woman like you. Regardless of where you are on your own path and journey, you are not alone in your dreams, and you are not alone in your fears.

It is in understanding the spiritual path we are on and embracing the human journey that brings us to our knees; the place where we find and face our greatest self and learn to reveal our own true voice. As we keep surrendering to this lifelong process of self-awareness and self-actualization, we discover how to share and reveal more of our true selves to create real and meaningful impact in the lives of others, both personally and professionally.

It is time for you to "Speak, Lead and Stay Feminine™"

As you embark upon the path to bring forward your unique self-expression, you will connect with what I assert is your deepest desire at a soul level (and perhaps something you have not yet said to anyone else): to share what is in your heart and be 'used fully' by God, Spirit, Source, Universe, or whatever your word is for your higher power. These are spiritual assertions, not religious ones.

Embracing the fullness of who you truly are as you discover and allow your purpose to unfold, allows you to become and share more of the real you. As you do this in earnest, you become more magnetic and available to have a real impact.

My hope, and the hopes of my co-authors, is that you find yourself in our stories. You find your voice in hearing ours. You find your true calling through us sharing ours. We are a community and this is a movement.

We are answering the call. We are leading a new conversation. We are waiting for you.

Will you join us?

About the Author, Tracey Trottenberg

If you have ever seen Tracey Trottenberg speak from a stage, then you know what effective communication, delivered from a place of authentic feminine power, looks and sounds like.

With over twenty-two years of experience in the corporate world and as an entrepreneur, keynote speaker, master trainer, and feminine leadership and conscious communication expert, Tracey has spoken to, trained, and coached tens of thousands of people internationally. Selected out of thousands, Tracey was a top-ten finalist of the prestigious "North America's Next Greatest Speaker" competition. She has shared the stage with luminaries such as Les Brown, Lisa Nichols, Marianne Williamson and more.

Whether leading workshops and retreats, working one on one or with teams, Tracey's work "starts where most people stop." She masterfully facilitates the inner work and fearlessly guides her clients and audiences to the depths of themselves. From there, she provides real-world strategies to "pull out the gold" and emerge with greater consciousness, confidence, and clarity to express their gifts and create real impact in the world. The style of leadership and communication that Tracey teaches creates immediate transformation among executives and their teams, small business owners, and individual entrepreneurs. She knows how to create trust, engagement, and an improved bottom line. Her clients have ranged from coaches, authors and speakers to business owners, entrepreneurs and million-dollar CEOs of large corporations and organizations, including Panasonic, Radisson Hotels and Resorts, Penton Media, Sprint Canada, Aruba Tourism Authority, BBDO, Leo Burnett, and many others.

Tracey is a rock star when it comes to teaching women how to "Speak, Lead, and Stay Feminine™." It oozes out of her pores, and she's taught thousands how to step into their authentic voice and own any stage.

Tracey founded Amazing Women International, Inc. (AWI) to create, train and showcase a community of feminine leaders and messengers. AWI specializes in coaching women entrepreneurs and executives to help them access the source of their own feminine power and authentic voice. Creating experiences and programs to teach "messenger training from the inside out" Tracey has dedicated her life to helping women find their "Feminine Leadership Sweetspot™".

A native of Montreal, Canada, Tracey shares life and the stage with her amazing husband - speaker, author, and producer, George Peter Kansas - delivering live event experiences for coaches, authors, entrepreneurs, teams, C-level execs and couples. She is the author of the paradigm-shifting eBook, "The Seven Secret Strategies of Feminine Leadership & Communication" and has been featured in the Huffington Post, Wall Street Journal, iVillage, and other media outlets. Along with George, she is the co-creator of "Own, Honor and Unleash™" and "Speak with Soul: Rock From the Stage™" live experiences, co-author of the upcoming book "The R.O.I. of Y.O.U.™" and co-host of "The Deeper Conversation™" podcast. Together with their cherished cat Stormy, they make Los Angeles home.

Tracey's personal mission is to end verbal and emotional abuse by changing the conversation that happens on the inside to create a more loving relationship with yourself and your inner child. From there, a more conscious communication naturally extends to every conversation and every 'stage', creating kinder conversations, and kinder behavior towards others, especially children and animals.

A Personal Message from Tracey Trottenberg

https://youtu.be/WZPrKoLrbRA

www.amazingwomen.org/faces

Connect with Tracey Trottenberg

You can find out more about Tracey Trottenberg and connect with her directly here:

Email: asktracey@amazingwomen.org

Websites: www.traceytrottenberg.com,
www.amazingwomen.org
www.speakwithsoul.com

Twitter: https://twitter.com/TraceyTrott

Facebook: https://www.facebook.com/tracey.
trottenberg

LinkedIn: https://www.linkedin.com/pub/tracey-
trottenberg/8/772/b39

About Amazing Women International, Inc.

Amazing Women International, Inc. (AWI) creates conscious conversations.

We lead the leaders who are here to create and lead new conversations in the 21st century. Conversations that are shaping the world we live in now, and those we will leave for our children.

It is our mission to help each woman recognize her full potential as a business leader, as a "messenger" and as a woman. To help her find fulfillment, both personally and professionally, and to make it safer for women to express themselves in the world.

We do this because we believe that the more safe the world is, the kinder we all are. Kinder to ourselves, kinder to our partners, kinder to our children, the animals and the planet. That's the legacy we desire to create and leave.

Our global reach has helped tens of thousands of entrepreneurs, corporations and governments embrace a higher consciousness and a higher and deeper conversation, thereby creating greater results and impact by doing so.

We are revolutionizing feminine leadership by teaching women how to make a positive change in their lives and the lives of others.

We provide the training, coaching, community and support they need to lead and speak from their authentic core and feminine strength, to create meaningful, sustainable results. Our programs are delivered through online training programs, live events and intimate group and one-on-one coaching.

We bridge the internal landscape with practical, interpersonal and business skill development that provides a customized approach to leadership, management and communication techniques uniquely designed for women.

Our community is a sacred environment for purposeful and professional women who desire to make a greater difference to express themselves more fully and freely, and discuss and transform their challenges and fears. In our safe and guided space, they are supported by like-minded, successful and spiritual women without fear of judgment or competition that they often find elsewhere.

We believe that "When one woman succeeds, we all succeed."

We also celebrate, educate and support the extraordinary men who hold space for their Amazing Women, through our parent organization, Amazing International. While it does indeed take a village to raise a child, it also takes an entire community to fan the flames of today's Amazing Women.

Amazing Women International, Inc. is the land upon which that community is being built!

In Gratitude to You

Voices for the Voiceless™

Thank you for your generosity in purchasing "Faces of The New Feminine Leadership: Real Women. Real Conversations. Real Impact."

Amazing Women International, Inc. shares a percentage of revenue from all of our programs and book sales with active charitable organizations dedicated to the passionate empowerment of women, vigorous protection of children, ethical and loving treatment of animals, compassionate support of cancer patients, caregivers and survivors, and the loving stewardship of our mother Earth. You're already using your voice for good and your dollars to give and help others!

We would be so grateful if you could take a minute or two to share what you loved about this book and provide an honest review on our Amazon sales page.